THE LITTLE INNOVATION BOOK

2ND EDITION

JAMES A. GARDNER

ISBN: 978-1-4461-4749-8

*To the innovators
around the world who have
shown me the way as
I learned my trade.*

Contents

Preface

THE AIM OF this book is to provide you with the smallest number of things you need to know to start building an innovation management capability that creates value in your organisation.

This is somewhat challenging, because innovation management is a relatively new discipline. It doesn't have the history of, say, marketing or accounting. As a result, there isn't really a body of practical experience which permits practitioners to say "this is the right way!". Instead, innovators are often forced to make it up as they go along.

Sometimes, what they've tried has worked, but more often than not, it hasn't. The result is innovation is seen as a discipline which lacks a little something in the way of credibility.

Some of us, though, have been working hard to create reliable and repeatable processes that work for large organisations. This has taken us on a journey that's led to an unmistakable conclusion: you must treat innovation as a business process, and it needs to earn its place amongst other mission critical processes - like marketing and accounting - in organisations.

The Little Innovation Book is a collection of essays based on my writing on innovation over the last four years. It encapsulates much of the learning I've had driving innovation in various large organisations such as Microsoft and Lloyds Banking Group, and attempts to distil this into a set of topics that anyone considering an innovation effort will find useful.

I hope you'll enjoy *The Little Innovation Book,* and that you find it useful in your innovation efforts. I certainly enjoyed the creative processes

Introduction

IT HAS BECOME obvious, in retrospect, that organisations with superb knowledge economy credentials – companies such as Microsoft and General Motors, for example – weathered the global economic crisis little better than companies based on the industrial age economics they superseded.

Industrial age economics revolve around the premise that organisations win if they have control of financial and physical assets. They are manufacturers, banks, and mining organisations. They are farmers and primary producers. They are the companies which, historically, have made nations great.

Knowledge economy companies are quite different. They recognise there is inherent value in know-how and intangible assets such as brand and goodwill. They prize patents and other intellectual property, and their value is based not on control of physical assets, but the quality of the talent they're able to hire and retain.

So why was it, then, these knowledge economy companies weren't better insulated from the downturn despite all their talent, knowledge, and intellectual assets?

Knowledge economy companies must be missing something.

Some analysts – myself included – have concluded the missing thing is Innovation Capital. Innovation capital accrues from the set of procedures, people, and infrastructures an organisation creates to translate knowledge into value.

Innovation capital is generated whenever organisations make investments which allow them to do things which aren't business-as-usual. As a result, they are very good at handling situations which are unexpected.

This is an explanation for the observation that many knowledge economy companies failed to do terribly well during the global economic crisis. Faced with unprecedented circumstances, they simply weren't prepared when their business-as-usual operations were subject to dramatic changes.

Apart from poor performance during the downturn, what is driving modern companies to shift to innovation economics?

Most economies are about consumption. Companies are measured on their success as a function of growth. Growth is dependent on selling increasing volumes of product and service, ultimately with the goal of controlling particular markets.

This works when there is relative scarcity of the goods and services needed to make life worthwhile. But individuals (in developed nations at least), increasingly have all the physical goods and services they need to live happy lives.

In other words, there is an upper limit beyond which consumption is no longer able to fuel corporate growth at the rates historically demanded by markets. Even population growth, which is slowing anyway, is no antidote.

The implication of this is simple. Corporate growth cannot be expected to continue indefinitely by encouraging consumers to do more of the same. A satisfied customer who has everything they need does not translate into sales.

Innovation economics are different, because fortunes are made by encouraging customers to embrace diversity, to do things in completely new ways. The basis of competition shifts from quality, brand and price, to discontinuities that capture the imagination.

It is to creating these discontinuities the innovation economy organisation dedicates itself. For evidence this works, one need not go much further than the queues which form whenever Apple, the mobile computer company, releases a new product.

But why do knowledge economy companies still exist at all, if consumption is no longer the driver it once was?

It has traditionally been thought that some kinds of products or services can be provided only by very large organisations with control over industrial age resources.

Bankers are bankers because they have millions to invest. Drug makers succeed because they have huge research and development facilities. Fast moving consumer goods companies win because they have supply chain capabilities that connect products to supermarket shelves.

These historical barriers to entry provide large organisations with the illusion that they're safe from the upstarts who are encroaching on their established operations. Because of the titanic investments *they* needed to enter markets in the past, they imagine that *any* entrant will need to make them also.

But the Internet and other technologies have changed that. Now, anyone can produce and distribute anything, without the scale investments needed previously.

Software can be produced in days. Companies started in minutes. Call centre operations leased on demand. There are even cheap three dimensional printing machines capable of producing industrial age products with little or no investment at all. Even shipping can be outsourced at any level of scale with reasonable economics.

In short, few traditional barriers to entry exist for either industrial or knowledge economy businesses any more. Anyone can compete with anyone, as long as they are creative, have a good idea, and the will to execute.

Those with less access to industrial and knowledge assets, however, are forced to compete immediately on the innovation front, and invariably proceed to do so without very many constraints.

Most large organisations have people who know this, and are quite aware of the threat posed by these nimble, small entrants. They know they have to do something, but their challenge is finding a critical mass of supporters inside their organisations who agree the threat is real.

Invariably, many companies find themselves being disrupted by the upstarts they thought were no threat to them. This happens insidiously. By the time enough people realise what has happened, it is often too late.

How do you prevent this occurring? One answer is instituting a systematic approach to value that searches out innovation from employees, customers and suppliers. Such an approach seeks to make it possible for creativity to flourish *and* to convert it into useful products and services. Generally, the latter part is the hardest.

This book contains 10 rules you can follow to create a value-enhancing innovation method of your own.

In Rule One we discuss the need for an innovation strategy. You'd be surprised how few new innovators recognise the need to have the end-goal in mind before they start. But if you don't know the destination, how can you design the journey?

Rules Two and Three are concerned with the nature of innovation and the roles you might expect innovators to take on. Both are important: the former, because knowing what innovation actually means in an organisational context makes it simpler to succeed, and the latter, because not everyone will agree at the beginning what those charged with finding innovation should actually be doing. Agreeing both up front is a shortcut to faster results.

Rule Four is about the money you need to invest. You'd be surprised how many organisations decide they want more innovation, but think of the money as afterthought. This is the section you should read to discover how much money you need, and how much money is too much.

In Rule Five, we'll examine three big myths about innovation. Most people think innovation is about finding big hits. They imagine that if you have more ideas, you'll also have more innovation. And, most especially, they believe that innovation is an inherently risky investment. This is the section that explains why these commonly held beliefs are wrong.

Rule Six examines the way your technology people respond to innovative propositions. It also provides some thoughts on how to manage technologists when they say "no!". This will likely be often if your organisation is structured around cost avoidance and stability of delivery, as most are.

Moving onto the processes you can use to drive more innovation out the door, Rule Seven explains the questions an innovation project should be able to answer before it starts, while Rule Eight is about the diagnostics you should apply to ensure you *stop* innovating in directions which won't create value.

Rules 9 and Ten are mainly about people, and about innovation people specifically. It is tempting to imagine that these highly prized, extremely creative individuals should be locked behind closed doors, the better to protect the competitive advantages they're building. This is wrong, and usually results in much less innovation getting done. It is also attractive to think if you hire only really creative, right-brain type people, you'll get great innovation outcomes. This is also incorrect. These last two chapters will explain why.

Some readers, no doubt, will now be asking whether it is possible to build a decent innovation programme with only these 10 rules. If it were so simple, they'll be wondering, why don't all companies excel at innovation economics?

The answer, of course, is innovators will never learn all they need by reading books alone. Each innovation team grows its capabilities in a specific way, for a specific organisation. This happens organically as they try things to see what works and what doesn't. The failures are as much a part of the learning as the successes.

Getting started is what counts, and where many companies find the greatest challenge. These 10 rules are signposts that get the innovation journey started.

For me, this book has also been a journey. Last year, I wrote a big, thick book on innovation programmes for the banking industry. People seemed to like the book, but they felt at almost 350 pages with tiny writing, there was way too much detail for those in a rush to start.

The *Little Innovation Book*, a much shorter volume, is my answer. The format is abbreviated, a suitable chapter-at-a-time read for the morning commute. I hope you find something valuable here.

So, let us get started. Turn the page and begin your own journey by deciding the innovation strategy your organisation will follow to leverage innovation economics.

Rule 1: Create an Innovation Strategy First

AN INNOVATION PROGRAMME has, on average, 18 months between the time it's initiated and cancellation. Most are cancelled because the innovators involved haven't generated results quickly enough.

What is the number one reason innovators fail to get timely results? Surely, it must be they didn't have a firm idea of what they were supposed to be achieving when they started.

You'd be surprised to discover the number of innovators with whom I discuss this who are unable to articulate their organisation's innovation strategy. You know you are dealing with a team in this category when you ask the question "Why does your organisation have an innovation programme?" and it takes more than a sentence to answer.

Deciding the overall objective of an innovation programme is the most fundamental, and most important, decision innovators and their sponsors will ever be asked to make.

It is a decision, though, that needn't be especially complicated, as there are really only three strategic options available from which to choose.

The first is obvious: don't do innovation at all. Rely on what worked in the past. Accept a "back to basics" approach is possible, and continuing practices appropriate a decade ago will, at least, let the business continue.

Some organisations have, indeed, adopted this strategy. It is a valid option, especially if what's needed is tight cost control for a few years. Those years may be used productively to rebuild balance sheets or customer bases, though it will be at the expense of building new capability to compete.

This may, or may not, be an option depending on the nature of the competitive situation an organisation faces. If there are strong competitors taking a leadership position in the market, abandoning innovation is hardly a sensible strategic move. On the other hand, if there is no burning platform driving an innovation agenda, what's to be gained by pushing it forward regardless?

Not doing innovation at all is a perfectly acceptable strategy, so long as everyone agrees up front.

The other end of the scale is Play-2-Win innovation. This is the innovation strategy you adopt when you can say, with no disagreement, "innovation is going to be the source of all competitive advantage in the future".

Innovators doing Play-2-Win are a relatively large investment in the short term, but (if they are any good) extremely profitable in the long term.

The kinds of investments one needs to make in a Play-2-Win situation can include corporate incubators, prototyping facilities, and other significant infrastructures. It's likely that returns, at least initially, will not be that large compared to the upfront costs of establishing the capability.

Because the upfront investment in capability can be so significant, innovators must be pretty certain they have the support needed to adopt this strategy before doing so. Their efforts will be front and centre of everything an organisation does from the moment this strategy is adopted, so they are highly visible when things go wrong. That is an uncomfortable place to be, and senior leadership must be ready to provide appropriate air cover.

As we'll see later in this book, things will almost always go wrong. Failure is a fact of life for innovation teams, and rates of 80% or more are not uncommon.

But not all failures are bad.

A good failure is one which teaches an organisation something. Usually, these lessons will be learnt after investment funds have already been committed. The best failures, therefore, are those where the lessons have been bought at the smallest possible cost. In other words, where the innovation team has cancelled a project early.

In a culture that celebrates good failures, the money spent on a stopped project is seen as an investment that can usefully support the innovation team in their future endeavours.

By contrast, a bad failure is one which fails to create new lessons at all. Bad failures are also typified by wasting significant amounts of money.

If it is hard enough to celebrate a good failure, you can imagine how difficult things become for an innovation team when they have to explain a series of bad failures. Usually, a string of bad failures results in the closure of an innovation programme altogether.

This is especially the case when an organisation has bet-the-bank on a Play-2-Win innovation strategy.

The third kind of innovation strategy is Play-Not-2-Lose. Play-Not-2-Lose accepts doing new things to maintain parity with competitors is the primary reason to have an innovation function. You may not get the market windfalls that accompany a big breakthrough, but you do get relatively good returns in the short term.

Even in an innovation economy, Play-Not-2-Lose can be very successful, because its main concern is the rapid improvement of that which an organisation does well now. In this strategy, innovators will typically concentrate on small, low risk changes, rather than big, grand, strategic projects. Compounded over time, Play-Not-2-Lose can generate massive increases in value.

Because each innovation is an incremental improvement on that which already exists, organisations tend to find Play-Not-2-Lose much easier to adopt than Play-2-Win. There are far fewer powerful people likely to be threatened. Then, too, the downside risk is usually small, on account of the fact that each individual innovation is probably not that significant in the overall scheme of things.

Deciding which of these three strategies to adopt is really a matter of determining the risk appetite of the organisation considering an innovation programme.

It is usually a mistake to adopt a Play-2-Win strategy when you work for an organisation interested in short term returns. As a rule, the kinds of grand projects required for execution of this strategy take longer than 18 months to germinate, the maximum time most innovation teams have as a grace period before hard questions about their value start to be asked.

Indeed, the temptation of new innovators to do Play-2-Win is one of the main reasons programmes fail. Spending time working on a planning horizon beyond the present vision of an organisation never ingratiates one to management.

Organisations wanting Play-2-Win, but looking for immediate returns from their innovation capabilities, are often in considerable distress.

Faced with a business in trouble, managers often imagine innovation may be a silver bullet capable of changing the game substantially enough all their troubles vanish.

For innovators, this is a poison chalice, because it doesn't take long for management to realise their expectations have little chance of being met. Their response is closure of the innovation team as soon as possible, usually as part of a "cost saving" exercise.

If your organisation can't be certain it wants to run a Play-2-Win strategy, it is perfectly appropriate to adopt Play-Not-2-Lose. Small, gradual, improvements done at scale are be a lucrative way to create a better business. Toyota, for example, used incremental improvements in their production processes to become one of the leading car companies in the world, not withstanding the quality control difficulties they faced in 2010.

Play-Not-2-Lose strategies are often derided by both innovators and their sponsors. The question asked is "what's the difference between incremental innovation and optimisation?". Why bother to have an innovation function if they are just doing the same work as other teams already engaged in the business?

But Play-Not-2-Lose is *not* the same as doing ordinary business-as-usual improvements of the kind popularised by methodologies such as Six-Sigma and Lean.

Lean and Six-Sigma are methods which take various levers available to managers, and through a systematic procedure, seek to determine the best possible combination to maximise a set of outputs. One might, for example, explore what combination of decisions and check points make best sense in a purchasing process.

Clearly, if there are too many of these checkpoints, everyone will be frustrated by how long it takes to buy anything. On the other hand, with no checks at all, an organisation might wind up buying things it has no use for.

Incremental innovation is quite different because it seeks to find new levers, rather than change the position of those that already exist. Lean or similar methodologies might be used later to optimise the positions of the levers, but it is innovation that creates them in the first place.

An organisation seeking to innovate its purchasing processes through innovation, for example, might explore crowd-souring methods for decisions-making, or reverse auctions for getting the best price, or any of an infinite number of other possibilities.

What the innovators would *not* do is work on fixing existing purchasing processes. Most organisations have teams that are specifically tasked with doing that kind of work, so it is clearly redundant for the innovation team to do it as well.

Of course, if there are no business improvement teams presently, it would certainly be a matter for innovators to propose that one be created.

In summary, then, the first thing a new innovation team (in conjunction with their executive sponsors, of course) must do is make a decision on which of the three strategies outlined here they'll adopt.

Everything that follows is determined by this key decision, from the infrastructures built to generate new value, to the influence innovators must ensure they create with stakeholders.

Let us now examine how a Play-2-Win strategy allowed a bank – the famously orange-coloured ING Direct – to disrupt every market it's entered since its inception in 1997.

Case Study

ING Direct Adopted a Play-2-Win Strategy when it first started in Canada.

From the start the proposition was unusual: a high interest savings account – a much higher rate than anywhere else in the market – in exchange for a reduction in the number of channels through which it could be accessed.

With the ING product, there were no expensive branches or ATMs, just rudimentary call centres and online access. Payments in and out of the account were done through the intermediary of other banks.

The introduction of this model in Canada was done in relative isolation from the ING parent company in the Netherlands, who by all accounts did not have much of an innovation strategy at all.

It is extremely doubtful whether the new model would have been allowed, in fact, had head office shown more than passing involvement in its germination: if it was successful, it would likely have cannibalised INGs core businesses which were much more traditional in execution.

Luckily, the geographical separation of Canada from Europe meant leaders of the new business had a much freer hand than they would have done otherwise. They were able to adopt a Play-2-Win strategy whilst working under-the-radar.

Under-the-radar is a topic we will come back to later in this book, but suffice to say, ING Direct was launched, initially without getting much attention from the Netherlands.

Direct banking is quite different to models most banks pursue when they acquire savings accounts. Usually, they focus on customer experience in a full range of channels, including expensive branch and call centres. The competitive differentiation is the quality of the customer journey, *not* the interest rate. This makes operating a savings account very expensive, and to preserve margins, banks kept interest rates low.

ING Direct turned this model on its head. It kept its *costs* low and handed over the savings to customers. The new account was a huge hit.

Disruption of the savings market in Canada was rapid.

With this success under its belt, the once-doubting ING head-office replicated the model in many other markets. In every case, the competitive landscape for savings was disrupted completely. Banks with high cost bases structured for competition on customer experience were forced to compete on price, whilst their existing customers continued to enjoy their expensive channels.

This is extremely painful for bankers faced with the arrival of direct banking, but the alternative is to lose deposit share altogether. As you might imagine, bankers are usually not delighted when they discover ING Direct is planning to enter a new market.

Rule 2: Define What Innovation Means

ALTHOUGH IT MAY sound obvious, defining the term "innovation" in the specific context of an organisation is one of the most important things new innovators can do.

You'd be surprised if you knew the number of innovation groups I've worked with who can't articulate a brief answer to this. They'll try various fluffy responses. These range from "attempting disruption of competitors" for teams with big ambitions, to "enhancing core operations with incremental improvements" for those less so.

Usually, there will be little consensus on the definition either amongst themselves, or with their sponsors.

Not infrequently, I've seen discussions go round the same arguments for so long that someone will suggest "we don't need a definition, lets just get on with it". This is a mistake.

Multiple divergent opinions on what you're trying to achieve in an innovation programme almost always leads to a situation where nothing is achieved at all. On the other hand, knowing the shape of success up front makes it much easier to execute whichever innovation strategy has been selected.

One common misconception is innovators should only engage in very large, transformational projects. As long as this is the agreed definition for an appropriate innovation effort, there is nothing wrong with this.

A problem arises, however, when innovators pursue a *balanced* portfolio without an appropriate definition of innovation available to them. Since many of the things attempted won't be transformational at all, inevitably some people will suggest this means the "innovators aren't innovating".

A definition of innovation which concentrates on very large, very strategic projects makes it impossible for innovators to do little things which help spread their risk. When you have all your eggs in one basket, there is a very high probability that *all* your projects will fail.

Most innovators know they will have one (or, if they are especially lucky, two) successes from every ten or more things they try. Sophisticated innovation managers, therefore, do many things at once. In order to spread their risk, they balance the set of projects they are supporting, mixing large strategic opportunities and small, incremental ones.

To be successful doing this, a broad definition of innovation applicable to any opportunities the innovation team might investigate is needed. Because the team will generally not know in advance how the next useful idea will arise, defining innovation prescriptively is usually counter-productive.

A further important characteristic of a good definition is it is careful to avoid threatening the interests of established business operations too much.

This is especially important. Established businesses in companies are usually very powerful. They have control of most of the resources, and they use them producing whatever-it-is that defines the organisation. They are key to the strategic mission, and will tend to feel justified acting in their own interest. Their own interest will tend to be doing things that preserve the status quo.

Innovators will, eventually, have to challenge the status quo if they are to do their jobs properly. Therefore, getting a definition which gives them flexibility to do so whilst balancing the risk they'll be shut down (for being distracting to core operations) is something that must be dealt with up front.

In innovation programmes I've been responsible for, we've successfully used the following:

Innovation is anything beyond business-as-usual.

Note this doesn't prescribe either the scale or volume of innovation that is undertaken. Innovators are free to do anything at all that is not already being done. But it does make it clear to everyone that if they already have something working, the innovators won't interfere.

It is a good balance between having flexibility and ensuring potentially affected stakeholders don't sabotage the innovation programme before it starts.

After "innovation", the next most word most likely to cause a definitional argument is "disruptive". Without fail, this is a word so charged with alternate interpretations that its use clouds any discussion almost immediately.

The most common misuse of the term "disruption" is its application to any product or service new enough it's not yet been copied by competitors. Those who use the term in this way reason that if they're doing something competitors are not, it must disadvantage them in some way. In other words, they are being "disrupted" by the activity.

Unfortunately, since it is usually possible for competitors to replicate most new things pretty quickly, any disruption that occurs is short lived.

True disruption occurs when advantages over a competitor are *not* easily replicable, circumstances which arise when one of the two following conditions exist:

The new product or service targets a customer segment unattractive to an incumbent. Normally, this will be either because margins are too thin to make the customer profitable, or the functionality provided by the incumbent is much greater than the customer can afford. In both cases, a disruptor with a small cost base can enter a market with something that is perfectly adequate for low-end customers and use this as a beach-head for expansion upward. Incumbents are generally unable to respond because their cost bases (and operational structures) are optimised to serve their customers at the high end of the market. This is the model pioneered by South West Airlines and Ryan Air.

The new product or service is a substitute for a high end offer a customer is already using, but provides only that set of capabilities the customer actually needs. In this case, a customer will switch to the disruptor's offering in order to avoid paying a premium for capabilities they don't use. Here, too, the incumbent is unable to respond. In order to serve its high end customers, it has to retain most of the expensive functionality which drives its cost base. Removal would jeopardise the high end customer segment, the source of most of the revenue, whilst provision of a lesser product would cause over served customers to switch, reducing net revenue. This is what has occurred to Microsoft with Office, whose features are used by at most 20% of its customers. Increasingly, Office is being replaced by free, online alternatives from firms such as Google.

In both these cases, the incumbent is under threat in the long term because the new player is able to do something the incumbent one can't. Disruption, in these instances, means a big company with an entrenched position can be overturned by a smaller one.

Sooner or later, disruption happens to all companies in all industries, which, of course, is one of the reasons firms need to be innovating from within. Their innovators are their protection against the future.

The seminal book describing disruption is Clayton Christensen's *Innovators Dilemma.* I suggest your review this text for more details on the mechanics of disruption, as well as some great case studies.

Of course it makes sense to do disruptive things if you're running an innovation programme and the opportunity to do so presents itself. However, innovators need to be cautious when attempting to do so, because there are two traps which must be avoided.

The first is disruptive innovations do not happen overnight. The processes involved in overturning an entrenched competitor (or an established business line internally) can take years. If an innovation programme wants to be disruptive, it must first ensure it has enough successes under its belt to prove its value until its disruptive investments pay off.

The second reason for caution is any situation where an innovation enters territory normally managed by an internal business group. Inevitably, innovators will spot opportunities they may wish to pursue inside their organisations. The problem is those responsible for current business will fight tooth and nail to prevent such innovation succeeding, because they know they will eventually lose control of their operations as the disruption begins to scale up.

This is rational behaviour. Most line of business managers spend their time working out how to prevent anyone disrupting their operations. The sensible behaviour for a manager facing a disruptor is to reinforce the successes of the past at the expense of the innovation. They are highly motivated to do so, since the alternative looks remarkably similar to failure.

In addition to the definitions I've already advanced for innovation, there are other subdivisions which can inform decisions on how an innovation team will spend their time. One of the most useful is categorisation of innovations based on how unprecedented they are compared to what has gone before.

The first category is innovation which is transformational, creating brand new revenue streams or defining new product types. Apple's iPad is such an innovation. It creates a new product category: a slate for personal online media consumption. Previous alternatives – personal music players and laptops - are functionally less good at this particular task than iPad with its big screen, touch interface, and attractive price.

Transformational products and services such as these are often described as radical or breakthrough innovations by analysts. They're extremely speculative, but have high returns if they're successful.

Many executives, when asking innovators to produce, do so with the expectation that they'll get radical innovation, but they want it without the risk of failure. This is pretty much impossible to achieve in any reliable way, and is one of the top reasons innovation teams get fired. Management always goes off the idea of systematic innovation when their hopes are dashed by big, visible failures at the start.

This is one of the reasons you'll find this book advocating innovation teams restrain their ambitions at the beginning.

Radical innovation is risky, and without a track record of success, very hard to explain when it goes wrong. A more reliable strategy is to start out with many incremental innovations, the sort we'll come to next.

Incremental innovations take what is already being done and enhances it in some way. Incremental innovations are enhancements along the well understood trajectory of traditional business as usual.

Such innovations have characteristics such as enhancing market reach (by adding features that make the product or service attractive to more customers), or supporting higher prices (through the addition of capabilities which create new value).

Incremental innovations, done in large numbers, can add materially to the growth of enterprises. They are also much less risky than radical innovations, since firms will usually have deep understanding and capability in the areas they address.

Most sophisticated innovation programmes create a portfolio of projects in both categories in order to balance their risk of failing to achieve decent overall returns. Many incremental, low risk innovations counter the expense of a few big failures and support the innovation programme until it is lucky enough to get a significant hit.

But this is not what *all* new innovation teams do.

Some innovation efforts start by riding high on the expectation they'll deliver amazing benefits in a short time. Sooner or later, stakeholders realise the "amazing" benefits are still some time away, and, frankly, might not be so amazing after all. Wracked with disappointment, they lose interest.

On the other hand, an innovation team which sets appropriate expectations up front does not have these difficulties. With stakeholder agreement to an innovation strategy (either Play-2-Win or Play-Not-2-Lose), *and* an agreed definition of what constitutes acceptable innovation, everyone is on the same page at the start.

Case Study

MICROSOFT OFFICE IS a great example of the power of incremental innovation to drive massive returns. Office, in 2009, accounted for about one third of all Microsoft's revenue. And, with penetration of the software approaching market saturation, Microsoft doesn't have very many new customers it can sell to.

What, then, is the secret of the financial success of Office?

Every few years, Microsoft releases a new version which contains many incremental improvements. There is usually nothing radical in each release (although Microsoft will argue this point, of course), but each adds functionality which is attractive to some segment of the existing customer base.

For a significant percentage, the new features are useful enough to justify an upgrade. An upgrade, in this case, means Microsoft is able to charge customers for the software again, albeit at a small discount to recognise the fact of previous ownership.

Unsurprisingly, adding all this capability has moved Microsoft firmly into a place where it is ripe for disruption.

There are now users for whom there are so many features it is impossible to get value from each one. With every upgrade, nonetheless, they are charged to use these unwanted features.

This is fertile territory for a player who is less capable and therefore less expensive. A less capable alternative might not satisfy that small segment of Office customers who use *all* the features of the software, but it will likely be *good enough* for most.

Customers such as these, indeed, are the market that Google and other Software-As-Service players are attempting to attract. Starting from a price of nothing, they offer less functionality than Office, but the subset that *is* available is sufficiently powerful that a good percentage of customers can switch without losing much.

With every release, the new online tools get better. As they do so, they come closer to matching the needs of more customers of Office.

There are few responses Microsoft can make which do not destroy its core revenue streams. If it creates a less capable version of Office, one which it can offer at a lower price, it risks cannibalising its own customer base.

If it does nothing, it will continue to lose customers to the web.

Economically, the most attractive option (to Microsoft managers) is to allow the low end customers to defect to the web, whilst creating new functions that allow the company to charge even more for features at the high end. This ensures the company can still grow its Office revenue, at least in the short term. This, of course, is the strategy the company is presently following.

Long term, unfortunately, it is a losing strategy. Web based products will eventually match Office on a feature by feature basis, at least for the core functionality that customers care about. With their much lower cost, customers will defect en-masse.

To save itself, Microsoft needs an innovation programme with the internal power to disrupt a core operation of the business. In this particular case, that would mean an internal group with the influence to sacrifice *one third* of the company's revenue in the interest of its long term future.

There are few signs that such a programme exists in the company.

Rule 3: Make Sure the Role of Innovators is Clear

KNOWING WHAT INNOVATION strategy is right for your organisation is important because it defines the purpose of an innovation effort. Getting a definition of innovation to which everyone will agree is equally important, as doing so sets the tactical boundaries innovators will stay within whilst they try to deliver the strategic goals that have been set.

But there's another thing you have to work out before you start innovating, and that's the kind of role you want the innovators to play. Are they active participants in the process of creating new things? Or are they, instead, the stewards of an "innovation culture" in which things happen without much central intervention. Indeed, is there really any need to have a formal group of innovators at all?

It is to these questions that we'll now direct our attention.

Firstly, let us examine the idea of an "innovation culture". The "culture" discussion is another of those thorny innovation issues which will probably engender significant argument in any organisation.

The question really boils down to this: is innovation part of everyone's day job, or is it something which should be handled by a central team?

Some argue a truly innovative company has a culture of support that ensures new things happen by themselves. In such organisations, the argument goes, you don't need a central innovation team at all, because individual employees are empowered and motivated to make the kinds of changes their firm needs to stay competitive.

To be honest, I am yet to see any organisation with a culture that does this.

Many companies who say they want an "innovation culture" fail to take active steps to make things happen. They imagine that, with creative enough employees, they will get innovation for free.

It's important to remember people have day jobs, and quite likely it is day-job activity on which they are measured. Unless you can couple innovation to these core activities, you'll probably get little more than lots of ideas that go nowhere fast.

This is very common. Managers expect innovation and encourage it via employee engagement events, or internal suggestion boxes, or other mechanisms. With their new innovation "initiative" launched, they fail to take the next step: the provision of a framework to support execution. Then, everyone wonders why their innovation efforts don't deliver.

Almost anyone can dream up great ideas, but there are far fewer people who actually have the skills to take those ideas and turn them into something useful to their organisations. By failing to address this fact, proponents of "culture" as the solution to "innovation" are making the suggestion that it's possible to get measurable and predictable results through what amounts, essentially, to doing nothing.

If you are going to have an "innovation culture", you must find ways to encourage employees as they pursue activities which are probably outside their formal performance management regime.

One role the innovation team can take on, then, is as the arbiters of the framework that supports an innovation culture. In this scenario, the innovation team fosters and manages an environment that supports other people in the firm who wish to be innovative.

Innovation teams taking the role of arbiters generally perform certain activities. They will likely provide skills training for employee, coaching them in methods they can use to attract funding for new propositions. They may deliver mentoring and guidance to managers who need to foster the innovations of their employees. And, most importantly, they'll probably provide insight for senior executives, who, busy with day to day operations, must be prompted to continually give their employees permission to do things out of the ordinary.

Such innovation teams have a considerable challenge in front of them, because although they do not directly control the outputs of the innovation process, they will certainly be measured on them. In most cases, if the role of the innovation team is to be an arbiter of culture, results will take quite a bit longer than when they participate in the process directly.

At the other end of the spectrum is a scenario where the innovation team is centrally involved in the generation of innovations themselves.

Central innovation teams are a model well adopted in many industries, from pharmaceuticals, where research and development budgets tends to be held by large business units dedicated to the purpose, to banking, where there are likely to be a few smaller new product development teams. Even in Government, there's increasing reliance on central innovation teams to drive efficiencies and cost savings.

It's easy to understand why. Central teams are easy to set up and much less difficult to measure than diffuse arrangements that rely on an "innovation culture. It is easy to point at them and say "that's how we're doing innovation". They make executives feel good about their innovation efforts, because when you can nominate specific individuals and assign accountability for actions, you know things are likely to get done.

Now, in this model, the innovation team is the group that decides how and when to innovate. They ordinarily control an investment budget of some kind, and are accountable for making investments that drive forward the innovation agenda. If they are any good at all, they will sign up to some big return numbers that can justify the money they're given.

But there's a problem with a central innovation team that does everything: in order to get more innovation, you have to add more people. This doesn't scale, and here is why.

For most new things, the difference in effort required to get an organisation to do something radical versus something a little more incremental isn't all that great. You still have to do all the influencing, the management of politics, and of course, the finding of the money.

Incremental innovations, though they tend to be relatively risk free compared to their radical cousins, don't generally make big returns individually. You need to be doing a lot of them before you make a sizable difference to any metrics which are material to the larger business as a whole. With a central team, you often find the individual incremental innovations don't pay for the time of the innovators.

By contrast, doing things which are more radical provides better returns, but at a much greater risk level. This makes it seem sensible for innovators to select radical innovations for their portfolio. Given the choice of almost certainly not breaking even, and at least the chance of a big payoff, most teams will select the latter.

Obviously, longer term, both choices lead to cancellation of an innovation programme, because the moment Innovation Euphoria wears off, stakeholders examine the opportunity costs of the innovation investment. In light of relatively paltry returns from an incrementally focused team, and potentially sizeable failure costs from a radically focused one, the business case for innovation may not stack up.

Innovation groups which have lasted the test of time have worked out they need the continuity that comes with making predictable returns for their firms. To do so, they generally create a portfolio at scale: large numbers of incremental innovations which pay the bills for a small number of radical ones.

Once teams recognise scale is the key to predictability, it is only a small step further to understanding that for most organisations, a central team responsible for everything to do with innovation probably isn't the best idea.

One answer advanced innovation teams generally arrive at is *participative innovation*. This is a model where much of the day to day work of getting an innovation from idea to production is done by the employees who came up with the idea in the first place.

The innovation team contributes by providing a framework for execution, usually embodied in some kind of self-service infrastructure that reduces their hands-on time to the lowest possible level. The team will tend to ramp up its involvement in the latter stages of progress, once it looks like the idea will go somewhere and just needs that final kick to be turned into something real.

By running innovation in this participative way, the central team is able to have involvement in far more projects simultaneously. Furthermore, the investment they must make in each innovation - certainly at the beginning at least - is much reduced. This gives them liberty to be involved in a significant percentage of the incremental ideas, as well as the big, game changing radical ones.

Leveraging participation in this way means the overall scope of control for a central innovation team increases geometrically - not linearly - with each new innovator added. This is a result of network effects. One new innovator can influence many more participative employees, who in turn influence their own workgroups to participate as well. In the end, you get far more done.

So much for the role innovators will play in the overall innovation process. The next question needing resolution is the choice of an individual to lead the team.

This is particularly important, because whether you are running a central innovation team with a participative agenda, or a distributed innovation function with a mandate to shepherd an innovation culture, everything that happens next will devolve from the particular mentality the innovation leader brings to the table.

One option is putting an entrepreneur in charge, someone with proven capability to start and run new ventures. Such an individual knows everything about working on a shoestring and matching limited resources to big problems. He or she has proof they can turn an idea into something that works, because they've done it before.

An alternative is hiring someone with lots of experience managing portfolios of projects but not much depth in the intricacies of making individual projects successful. Someone who's more like an investor than a project manager.

Most people, given this choice, would hire the entrepreneur before the investor, reasoning the former will at least drive successful outcomes in the few things they choose to focus on. It seems an easy, low risk choice.

But the easy choice is not always the best choice.

Entrepreneurial innovation leaders are always highly motivated to make a few pet projects successful. That is how they've made a name for themselves in the first place, generally. They've taken a good idea, and through personal heroics, made it into something worthwhile. Usually, their whole careers have been built on a few lucky breaks, backed up with solid, long term effort.

Individual heroics are all very well, but most things innovators try will not work no matter how much effort is invested. The entrepreneur accepts this, and knows they should quit at an appropriate moment in order to start working on their next big thing. They live in the hope that *this* time they will have a big success.

For an innovation leader in a corporate organisation, though, this is potentially the worst strategy possible. Because innovation programmes last about 18 months, driving a small number of projects sequentially means you run out of time way before you have decent results.

I once worked with an innovation team where everyone was working on only three big ideas. Now, individually, each of these ideas was fantastic, potentially disruptive, even. There was every chance they'd succeed with a little bit of luck. Great ideas, good execution and a little bit of luck is all that any innovation really needs to be successful, actually.

But it is the luck part which is the problem. Whilst you can control - to a degree anyway - the ideas and the execution, luck is entirely random.

Unfortunately, despite everything (including massive individual heroics), the three ideas didn't turn out so well. One didn't scale to decent revenue quickly enough, so it was cancelled. The second, though it started to create good returns, was terminated because it became obvious it was cannibalising existing business. The third, sadly, got cut because the innovators stepped on the toes of someone important by accident.

All these cancellations made the team look like they weren't creating value. It was an easy choice for the firm to cancel the whole programme the next time it was necessary to find cost savings.

This story illustrates why hiring someone with an investment mentality is a good idea. Such individuals have an intuitive understanding of the fact that the real game in innovation is avoiding concentrations of risk. Three big ideas are much more risky than 30 small ones, especially when you consider most innovation teams average 1 success for every ten things they try.

Case Study

At the Department for Work and Pensions in the United Kingdom the innovation team is building a participative innovation framework. The idea is connecting employee ideas with systems that permit those same employees be innovative themselves.

This approach is relatively recent. Previously, the innovation team adopted a very centralised model, where it was accountable in its own right for developing unique propositions, without much in the way of interaction with anyone else. As is usually the case for teams working this way, the innovators suffered scale issues: they were only able to work on a few new things at once, proportionate directly to the number of people assigned to the team.

In 2009, however, the landscape changed. It was increasingly clear that traditional approaches to cost cutting and efficiency generation would not, in themselves, result in the kinds of savings the Department needed in the wake of the global financial crisis.

The innovation team were asked to ramp up their efforts to find radical ways of doing things. Some additional resources were provided to them, but it was obvious the old approach wasn't going to scale up to big enough returns to meet the challenge on the table.

Moving as much of the innovation process to the employees with the best ideas seemed an obvious way to get more to happen, more quickly. One of the main tools employed is a web site the team calls "Idea Street".

Idea Street is a web site on which employees can leave their ideas, vote on the ideas of others, and communicate in a very interactive way with everyone else in the Department who has something positive to add.

Those ideas voted highly by the community are usually the ones the innovation team spends its time working on. By the time they're doing so, an employee led team will generally have formed around the idea, and the input from the innovators is more in the way of guidance and support, rather than direct interventions.

Early results from this approach have been overwhelmingly positive. Employees have responded in a highly engaged way, going so far as to work on their projects outside their normal hours of work.

The biggest advantage of participative innovation at the Department, however, has proven to be the breadth of ideas captured, which range from minor operational changes to wholesale reform of core business. This diversity has provided the innovation team with fertile ground from which to construct a portfolio of activity.

Rule 4: Have a Connection to the Money

HOW DO YOU measure the results of an innovation programme? Do you count the number of new ideas you generate? How about the number of things your innovation team has worked on, or the number of new product introductions they've made?

These are useful measures, but don't justify the existence of an innovation programme by themselves. There is only one thing that will do that: a connection to financial results.

This is true whether you are running an innovation effort in the private sector (in which case you will be about creating new revenue), or the public sector (with a financial measure around cost savings).

For most innovators, the financial hurdle they need to reach is quite simple: the portfolio of projects selected must recoup the operating costs of the innovation team, and return a premium above attractive enough to divert investment from the (perceived) safety of business-as-usual.

Consider a scenario where an organisation can choose to invest in, say, a Lean initiative on one hand, or an innovation programme on the other. Let us imagine the Lean initiative will result in a 20% return on investment as bloated processes are thinned down and operational efficiencies are found.

Excluding their operating costs, innovators must find ways of making *at least* a 20% return on their efforts to be attractive for investment. This, however, is more challenging than it first appears for several reasons.

Firstly, it is probable that 8 of ten things innovators try will fail. This is a quite good success rate, actually, but has implications for financial returns – the two successful innovations must return enough to cover the costs of these failures. In other words, the two successes will have to go a lot further than their 10% contribution each if the innovation team is to be considered a better investment than Lean.

Secondly, the innovation team will have a challenge of timing.

The Lean investment starts making financial returns immediately. Innovations, however, rarely deliver so quickly. Genuinely new things take a while to catch on. It is an unusual innovation which can cover its costs in the same year as investment is made.

The two successful innovations, then, will only be favourably compared to Lean if they ramp up to big returns quickly.

All this makes it look as if a Lean programme will be more certain than an innovation investment. As you can see, justifying innovation in terms of returns can be challenging.

So difficult can it be to get a reasonable comparison in situations such as these, innovation teams often retreat to "mushy" metrics such as number of ideas captured, speed of idea development, or any number of other non-financial measures.

They get away with doing so for a limited period of time, but sooner or later, they'll be called to account. Previously excited stakeholders will start to ask what they're getting for the money they're committing. They'll begin to wonder whether they might have gotten better outcomes by investing in, as we saw, something like a Lean initiative.

This will likely happen inside the first year and a half, and innovators will be asked to justify their budgets. Though everyone will agree the team has done "valuable work", the only justification anyone will really consider valid is the financial one.

In any event, if all other available investment opportunities *can* justify themselves financially, and it is only innovations that can't, it is obvious where a rational business manager will direct future funding. This is especially true during a downturn, or any other time an organisation is under stress.

So innovators need to pay their own way if their programmes are to exist in the long term.

Some innovations, of course, do not have financial returns at all. For example, productivity improvements, particularly those based on information technology, often don't have real money returns. Obviously, there may be a lot of value in doing such things, and a sophisticated innovation programme will certainly pursue them, regardless of the likelihood of getting them to pay.

How, then, does an innovation programme with an overall imperative to make excellent returns find a way to work on things which don't make any money at all?

The answer is it must have a portfolio of innovations, most which pay, and some which don't. There will need to be more of the former, of course, and the obvious implication is the innovation team would certainly de-prioritise those innovations without decent financial returns until it has paid the bills.

The observation that you need to make reasonable returns on any money invested in an innovation effort leads to a further question: how much up-front investment does a young innovation programme need to get started?

The natural temptation is to ask for as much money as possible. In other parts of most organisations, having more money means you have more control, more chance of doing big things.

But control of a big budget is a mistake for new innovation teams because it makes it certain they will miss expectations substantially. Here is the reason.

When you start innovation projects, especially if they are more radical than incremental, the delay between investment and revenue can be protracted.

Let us take another hypothetical example. Let's imagine the best investment available to an organisation has returns of 49% in year one. That's unrealistic, I realise, but I use the number to illustrate the point.

Let's further imagine the innovation programme is spending a million a year in cash. In order to beat the best available alternative, they need to return 50% on their investments in year one. If the innovation team has made ten 100k investments in that year, and their (relatively standard) failure rate is 80%, the team needs to deliver two projects with returns of 750k each in the first year.

This is not really a very big ask: often you can do such a thing with a few properly screened innovations that touch high volume transactional processes in incremental ways.

Now let us imagine a much bigger programme, say one with 10 million or so to spend.

To get to 15 million in returns (assuming the same success rate as before), you'd need to make a hundred 100k investments. The twenty investments that succeeded would each need to return at least 750k.

However, a starting-out innovation team is simply not going to have the bandwidth to run a hundred small projects at once. They have no choice but to reduce the number of investments, and concentrate on much bigger projects.

Given that, then, let us say the innovators make ten investments of a million each. Now, in order to be better than the best available alternative investment, 2 of those ten investments have to return 7.5 million in the first year.

Now, you'll recall earlier I pointed out that most genuinely new things take a while to ramp up to decent returns. Potential adopters of innovations take time to make their decisions about whether to proceed or not, and usually they'll want to hear positive messages from people they trust before they do so. This doesn't happen quickly, at least at the start.

In fact, the only innovations which ramp up to massive returns quickly are those very, very few products which are hits. iPad and iPhone were hits. The movie *Avatar* was a hit. The drug Viagra was a hit. But by far the majority of new introductions come nowhere close to the take up of these examples. The ordinary course to profitability is much more protracted.

What is the chance of having two hit products from ten investments? Very slim indeed.

In almost every case, it is better to ask for less money and grow slowly to the point where it *is* possible to do a hundred projects at once.

The challenges faced by a large-budget innovation programme do not stop there, however.

Because such a programme must do things at scale immediately, it will come to the immediate notice of those who run the primary operations of the firm. Moreover, the innovation team is likely to conclude (given their inability to guarantee the hits they need to make their numbers), they should invest in projects which touch core operations in fundamental ways.

There will be an immediate backlash from the core when this occurs. As I've mentioned previously, rational managers accountable for these operations are highly motivated to ensure nothing is done to change the status quo. In their fight back against the innovators, they have powerful weapons available to them. If nothing else, they are able to point to the high failure rate on innovation projects as evidence they should be closed down. Their arguments will be particularly cogent, given the fact any competent firm will execute its core operations perfectly most of the time.

Considering all this, it is much simpler to start an innovation programme with smaller budgets, because the possibility of making decent returns is much greater.

Is it reasonable that innovation be compared to mainline business operations already established? Of course it is: a rational business leader will always prioritise investments that support current revenues and opportunities, and will do so because this leads to the lowest risk level for the organisation.

Innovation, on the other hand, is uncertain and (at least perceived to be) risky. Whether the innovation team likes it or not, this fact makes it significantly less likely that money will be available. This will be even truer if something happens to the executive sponsor who started the innovation effort in the first place.

Such sponsorship is one of the prerequisites for long term success, by the way. Given the great difficulty in justifying a large innovation budget in purely financial terms, the protection of a powerful sponsor is needed to ensure toleration for investments that look – on paper – to be less attractive than available alternatives.

Unfortunately, big people in big jobs do, generally, change responsibilities and roles ever 18 months or so. When that happens, the full force of business prioritisation hits almost immediately. The next guy wants to make his or her mark, and killing "risky" stuff that was a holdover from the previous incumbent is easy.

What all this discussion really boils down to, in the end, is the number one priority for innovators once they've started innovating, is to prove that though their activity has uncertain outcomes in comparison to core business, the returns they generate are eminently predictable and worthy of investment.

Running a portfolio of innovations is the best way to do this. Portfolios of innovations, just as portfolios of stocks and shares, are much more predictable than the individual components that comprise them.

But getting to predictability leads innovators to another key question: if you have a dollar to invest, do you take a gamble with a single radical innovation that might pay off hugely? Or is it better to take a more cautious approach that leads to returns way more modest, but practically certain?

If one looks only at managing the concentration of risk, you're better off doing many small innovations. Since innovation is a risky activity, it is certain a large percentage of what's started will fail. For most firms the failure rate is between 80% and 90%, though it can be considerably higher in some industries.

The key to managing this appropriately is ensuring all these failures are good failures: failures that don't cost very much and teach innovators a lesson they can use in the next innovation.

But failure is still failure, and it still costs money. By doing many small things in parallel, the innovation team is able to pay for their failure majority with those small numbers of things which are big successes.

The difficulty with this approach, unfortunately, is that it all takes time. Firstly, there's the need to build up the systems and processes which allow the innovation team to do all those things at once. And secondly, unless the innovators can be certain of their sponsorship (and therefore political protection), they have only 18 months to generate returns which will meet the long term success hurdle we've been discussing in this section.

These factors mean that in practicality, innovators who are starting up have to take some bigger risks than they might like to. If one had all the time in the world, the rational course would be a concentration on incremental innovations at scale, with the prospect of growing organically into more radical projects when the bills are all paid.

The new innovation team is in a race against time, however. It will, therefore, need to pick a few more radical projects to engage in if it is to ensure it scales up to the returns it needs.

It is impossible to give very many guidelines on which radical innovations should be pursued, of course, but there are two things which are absolutely certain.

The first is doing radical innovation is both more risky and more expensive than incremental. New innovators, therefore, should exercise caution and choose the *least* ambitious of their potential projects which have a reasonable chance of success.

The second, obviously, is ensuring not all the eggs are in one basket. Multiple radical innovations should be added to the portfolio, since running only one will almost certainly result in failure. In other words, innovators should choose the *least* expensive of their radical options, to ensure they have the headroom to do as many as possible.

So far, we've considered the situation of innovators with too much money, and innovators who fail to get reasonable financial returns. There is one last scenario which is important, and that's the one where the innovation team has no budget at all.

This is surprisingly common. Management, especially those who are proponents of innovation culture, feel all it takes to get more innovation is the assignment of a couple of people to the task. In many organisations, in fact, finding people is much easier than finding money, so this seems like an easy way to get an innovation effort started.

The problem, of course, is making innovation happen is not just about people and ideas. Execution, which is the difference between having an idea that just sits around, and having an idea which can actually be converted into something useful costs money.

How much money is really dependent on the funding approach that's applied to the innovation team, and there seems to be two major models around that are effective.

In the first, the innovation team is assigned a small "seed" budget, an amount of money they can use to try out a few things. If their experiments look promising, they are then expected to win the money to take things further from big budget holders, who have to be convinced of the value of their work before they invest. By far, this is the most common model.

The second model is one where innovators have all the money they need in their own right. They can choose to invest, or not, as they see fit. Such a model, of course, implies much larger budgets, with all the dangers we've examined already.

However, the situation where the innovators have no budget at all results in certain failure, and here's the reason.

Before anyone can make an investment decision in something new, there are three key questions to be answered.

The first is "Can we do this?", and is really technical: are the technologies, production capabilities, management systems, and other artefacts needed to create the innovation available? If not, can they be created at a reasonable price?

To answer this question, innovation teams will likely have to pay for research, for prototypes, and for the time of analysts. It is a rare innovation group that has every skill it needs in-house.

The second key question is "Should we do this?" which really boils down to economics. Before an investment decision can be made, sponsors have to know what the likely costs of the innovation are going to be, how much revenue it will generate (or new efficiency savings, for public sector organisations), and over what time frame they will occur. Unless financial analysts are part of the innovation team, they will either have to be borrowed from someone else, or their services paid for.

The final key question is "When?". This question is, perhaps, the most difficult of all to answer, because it seeks to understand the probable reaction of those affected by the innovation. For starters, innovators need to know whether people are ready to adopt whatever-it-is, because throwing an innovation at an audience who really have little interest is an expensive way to fail.

They also have to predict the likely reaction of competitors: clearly if the business case for an innovation is predicated on the premise that no other organisations will be able to duplicate the functionality for some period of time, it is a rather unfortunate situation if competitors respond unexpectedly quickly.

To answer questions such as these, there will likely be input needed by marketers, by competitive analysts, and even firms that specialise in knowing what competitors are doing. Once again, this all costs money.

For innovators with no money at all, there are few alternatives but to try to answer the key questions themselves.

Unsurprisingly, this results in poor business cases which are unattractive to big budget holders on account of their paucity of detail. The innovators wind up tossing poorly formed propositions over the fence for funding, with little or no chance of being taken seriously.

Reflecting back on the discussion in this section, it is possible to boil down the financial arrangements of an innovation effort to three big things that must be sorted out early.

Firstly, innovators need to make sure they're able to justify the investment money they get by making sure they are the best available investment around. Secondly, they have to be sure they don't get too much money at the start, because new innovation teams simply can't handle the volume needed to develop decent returns at scale without taking unacceptable risks. And finally, they need to consider the funding model their firms adopt for innovation, and if it's one where there's no funding at all, the best course is to call off innovation altogether.

Case Study

IF YOU WANTED an example of the challenges involved in scaling an innovation programme to make decent financial returns, they do not come much better than Proctor and Gamble, the global consumer products giant.

Proctor and Gamble are an example of a company with a Play-2-Win innovation strategy. They know most of their future successes will be driven by innovation activities, as they have been throughout the long history of the company.

Proctor and Gamble competes in fast moving consumer goods across five major categories, and invests most of its effort finding unique, innovative propositions that will build huge global brands.

Most large organisations, if they wish to satisfy demanding shareholders, need to generate growth of between 4 and 6 percent. For Proctor and Gamble, that is equivalent to innovation worth almost $4 billion a year.

By the year 2000, Proctor and Gamble were realising traditional innovation processes, comprising very capital-intensive internal research and development, were never going to be able to keep up with growth demands of this magnitude.

Analysis of the company's historical innovation performance showed the capital needed to create growth was increasing at a faster rate than the returns its investments were generating. It was fast approaching an inflection point beyond which further investments would have negligible impact on the fortunes of the company. Not an especially enviable situation for senior leadership, who realised they had to do something significant.

The fundamental issue was Proctor and Gamble had 7500 researchers driving their innovation efforts, but each additional one they hired was delivering incrementally less. The declining return on innovation was the reason capital spending was outstripping returns.

As we've seen already, when an innovation team is responsible for everything, you tend to get scale issues. You have to put more resources into a programme to get more results, but in the case of Proctor and Gamble even continual, sustained investment could not outpace the market's demand for growth.

Their response was itself, innovative. They decided to involve not only their researchers, but everyone else they had any relationship with in their innovation effort.

In doing so, Proctor and Gamble were pioneers of a very radical concept, now known as Open Innovation.

Open Innovation is the strategy adopted when you recognise you have a great deal of intellectual property which is valuable, but presently unused. Similarly, competitors and partners may have assets they aren't using either, but which may be useful to you. The open exchange of these for fair value is the core proposition of Open Innovation, and often results in significant value for both sides.

By the end of 2000, Proctor and Gamble had made a decision they'd aim to have 50% of their innovations sourced from outside the company. It made complete sense, since their internal estimates suggested there were at least 200 researchers available outside the company for every scientist within it.

The idea was not to replace the 7500 researchers owned directly by Proctor and Gamble, but to multiply their efforts by leveraging the work of the 1.5 million scientists outside the company.

There have been dramatic results. The company's innovation success rate has doubled. Overall investment in innovation activities has decreased from 4.8% to 3.4% of sales. But research productivity has increased 60%, and the company has a portfolio of 22 billion-dollar brands.

The result - a financial one - is Proctor and Gamble has seen its stock price double in the years since it made its decision to open its innovation efforts to the public.

Rule 5: Address the Three Big Myths

AS YOU GET an innovation effort up and running, you will most certainly come across a number of beliefs about the process which are incorrect.

Time and time again three big preconceptions will rear their heads. It is a good idea to deal with these up front: doing so will avoid considerable hassle for everyone later when expectations are missed.

The three biggest myths about innovation are these. Firstly, the belief that ideas are the most important thing, and if you have more of them you'll get more innovation.

The second big myth is that the point of doing innovation is to create big product hits, and that if you don't achieve them, the innovation effort is a failure.

The final myth is innovation is risky and unpredictable, and therefore a luxury best afforded only in times of plenty.

We've already touched on some of these myths in this book, but let us now examine them in more detail.

It is certainly true that having fresh, new ideas is very important if you want to have a decent innovation programme. Without ideas, after all, you don't have anything. But the problem is most people forget it takes more than great ideas if you want something that's actually valuable to customers.

You also need a process that's able to turn ideas into real products, services or process improvements. The execution part is where the hard work starts.

The reason people forget this important detail is simple: the process of generating new ideas is inherently creative. It's fun, leaving a feeling of accomplishment just because you've dreamed up something unique.

Everyone has had the experience of an energising brainstorming session resulting in full whiteboards: you leave the room satisfied you've done something amazing.

Much of the time, though, nothing further ever happens. People are so pleased with what they've dreamed up they allow themselves to forget there's still much more to do.

Then, when someone else not only has the same idea, but executes it well, there is universal teeth gnashing as people wonder "why didn't we do that?"

I, personally, have had this experience.

My colleagues and I imagined what it might be like if a bank website could reach into any other bank's web sites to scrape out transaction details. Then, all the details any customer could care about might be seen on a single web page. We sat on the idea, and were later gutted when present-day market leader Yodlee executed the same concept.

This story is illustrative of something else which is interesting about ideas, and that is they are rarely unique.

Ideas are a creative response to a problem without a present-day solution. People dream them up as they wonder what they might do to solve their problems, and they draw on inspirations from their environments around them to do so.

What people forget is neither their problems, nor the inspirations from which they draw solutions, are exclusively theirs. Someone else is likely to face almost the same challenges, and will likely come up with similar solutions.

This is why you find concepts arising in multiple places at the same time, even though the creative groups who came up with the ideas in the first place don't know each other at all.

When this happens, and it almost always happens, the differentiating factor is not the idea itself, but how much execution is put behind it.

In my previous example, my team and I lacked execution and did nothing with our idea. But Yodlee had plenty of execution capability. They remain market leaders, a position they have held from the very day they created the product category.

Even if you have excellent ideas and great execution, one must still deal with the perception that the only innovations that matter are those which create hit products. If ideas aren't key and execution is everything, the thinking goes, surely it makes sense to concentrate limited resources on a few big investments with potential to drive windfall returns.

This, of course, is a strategy that's been followed by Apple and other companies who are *perceived* to be innovative.

First, Apple released iPod, a massive hit that redefined the way that music is sold. Then it released iPhone, a device which redefined the way people expect to use their mobile phone. And recently, it released iPad, which is changing the way customers acquire and use the products of the liberal arts.

With a track record of success such as these, it is very hard for anyone to argue that doing massive, hit-product type innovation can be very, very successful. After all, Apple has now overtaken Microsoft in market capitalisation, a feat they achieved using a mere fraction of the resources Microsoft devotes to research and development.

The thing is, though, that for every one of Apple's big hits, there have also been major failures.

Before it launched iPad, it also had Newton, another personal device that failed dismally in the market. Before it had Macintosh, there was Lisa which was technically superior, but sold so poorly the company eventually dumped its excess stock into landfill to get a tax break. And more recently, there's been Apple TV, which Steve Jobs himself has described as a "hobby", a product which hasn't (at least at this stage) radically redefined anything very much.

The point is Apple has taken some pretty big risks, and it has had its share of bad outcomes.

But those who look at companies like Apple with their string of hits always conveniently forget failures still happen to everyone, and they happen with a regularity that makes focusing on big hits a very risky business.

The reality is Apple spends a lot of time in between its big hits doing traditional product development around incremental innovation. Things like Time Machine, which does backup. Or Airport Express, which makes it easy to set up wireless networks. Boring products which help to pay the bills.

As we've discussed elsewhere in this book, a balanced innovation portfolio never focuses on big, transformational change to the exclusion of all else, because doing so results in very significant concentrations of risk.

Since innovators have about 18 months to develop decent returns before management gets bored, concentrating risk is a very hit or miss affair. You might get lucky, but if your future career is on the line, why would you take a risk which is substantially unnecessary?

There are, in fact, a number of companies which have made very good businesses out of doing incremental, rather than radical, innovation. Toyota, for example (prior to its recent product recall scandal) built itself into the largest car manufacturing firm in the world with laser-like concentration on small incremental changes.

Even Google, the search behemoth, is a company that has kept itself current by incremental innovation. Disregarding the business model change of pay-per-click advertising (which it didn't invent, by the way, but did make successful), Google has spent most of its time making small improvements to the one thing it does very well.

PageRank, the algorithm that first propelled the company's success by making Google results better than competitors, was only an incremental improvement on the search engines of the time. Google has continued its leadership in the area, though, by tweaking and enhancing what it already knows how to do. It has proved a very successful strategy indeed.

Of course, it's impossible to ignore that big hits have been very successful for some firms. And not *all* those firms have had to invest in the long series of failures that Apple, for example, has done before generating the golden hits which have made their fortunes. Such firms have been very, very lucky.

Some say buying a lottery ticket is an idiot-tax. People buy in the hope they'll win, then need do nothing to ensure returns except pass loose change across a counter. Naturally, they are disappointed when, in by far the greatest number of cases, they don't make much money.

Focusing on radical innovations in the hope of hits is an idiot tax on your business. Why on earth would you leave something to luck when you can reduce risk by creating a balanced portfolio of innovations with both incremental and radical components?

The good news is you don't have to do all that much incremental stuff before the dividends start to arrive (remember, the chance of failure for incremental innovation is quite low), and these will pay for the risk of doing radical innovations.

It is inevitable, though, that when you tell management they're not likely get big, transformational projects at the start, they'll think something funny is going on. Didn't they support innovation in the first place so they could get big results?

It is important to help them understand your innovation effort has ambitions, but will take time to build up a capability to the point where it is possible to do big things with some level of reliability.

The third big myth follows from the previous point.

Management, who have likely watched failed innovation efforts of competitors, or even worse, presided over failures of their own, may come to the conclusion that the risks of doing innovation are high. Taking such risks, they may decide, is justified only when times are good. At such times, there's money to spare, so wasting a bit on something speculative doesn't seem so silly.

The idea that innovation is speculative and risky is usually a sign that someone has experienced significant innovation trauma in the past.

Innovation trauma occurs whenever an organisation tries to do something new and fails at it so badly everyone decides the only safe course for the future is returning to business-as-usual. The result is organisations stagnate because they are so fearful they'll repeat their previous errors.

Sun Microsystems, now part of Oracle, is a good example. They released a device called *SunRay*, essentially a network computer, one quite ahead of its time.

SunRay promised to dramatically reduce the amount organisations would spend on technology. It would make everything simpler, easier to use, and more flexible.

When SunRay finally arrived, it did very few of these things, and customers turned on Sun's salespeople. Feeling the pain in their hip-pocket, the sales force then refused to have anything to do with many of the other new products the company created. They insisted on evidence of performance and capability before they would risk embarrassment in front of their customers again. Sun was hamstrung for years as a result.

Whether or not there are signs of innovation trauma, one thing is certain. People will not usually believe innovation can create decent returns reliably until they are shown it is possible to do so.

I cannot reinforce enough how valuable dealing with the three big innovation myths early can be. If you do so, the chance your innovation efforts will miss expectations is very much reduced. If you don't, however, management will almost certainly be disappointed quickly. The consequence of such disappointment is, at best, that further innovation success will be much harder to achieve.

Rule 6: Manage the Technologists

NO MATTER WHAT innovation strategy you've selected, and regardless the innovations that strategy leads you to consider, you will inevitably have to accommodate information technology professionals at some time during the process.

Information technology is a central and critical driver of production in almost all industries these days. This is true for activities dominated by industrial age economics as much as the emerging innovation economy companies taking the lead presently.

Because information technology is so important to much innovators do, the specific behaviours of IT folks has a very direct influence on how successful any innovation effort is.

In some IT organisations, there will be very strong opposition to any encroachment by innovators. Usually, this occurs in cases where IT is struggling with its business-as-usual responsibilities for some reason.

On the other hand, IT organisations can sometimes embrace innovation, even going so far as to create their own innovation teams so they can have something strategic to talk about with their business colleagues.

Regardless of the way your technology group behaves, however, there is one thing innovation teams will find impossible to avoid: the extreme emphasis many IT groups place on minimising change. As we'll see in a moment, there are good reasons for this behaviour. Unfortunately, though, it is an anathema to innovators, whose whole role it is to *create* productive, valuable change.

Most large companies with big IT infrastructures have teams whose sole purpose in life is to make it as difficult as possible to change things. They rationalise their existence using lines such as "we are here to protect service" or "uptime is our number one priority". They aren't bad people, but they have been programmed to do whatever it takes to reduce the risk of failure by their management. The best way to decrease the chance of such failures is to allow no one to touch anything in the first place.

For those times when change is impossible to avoid, there will be various governance processes in place, designed to make things as difficult as possible. This is usually deliberate. If a change is so necessary, then those responsible won't have any difficulty putting up with the mountains of process, the paper work and the hours of reviews before it is allowed, right?

Just why is it information technology organisations don't like change? For the answer, we must first examine the priorities of the Chief Information Officer, as handed out to him or her by the board.

Firstly, CIOs are concerned with making sure what they have right now is working properly. This is usually no mean feat, since they are often burdened with years, maybe even decades, of old computer systems. Despite their age, it is these old systems which drive current operations. The failure of even one usually causes massive repercussions.

Most CIOs have heard too many stories of organisations brought to their knees by computer failures to take any unnecessary chances they don't have to.

All these old, dated systems are expensive to run, and even more expensive to maintain. Some estimates, in fact, put total costs at greater than 80% of the entire IT budget.

How come it gets so expensive to keep dated systems running?

The answer is obvious when you examine the reasons systems fail.

Failures come in only a few flavours, the first of which is unintended consequences from change.

When anyone changes a computer in a large organisation, the impact can be far reaching. Every server tends to be related to many others in some way, resulting in a web of complexity which must be considered every time a change is done.

Now, because some of these changes affect systems which have been in place for years, it is highly unlikely that any one employee will have personal knowledge of *everything* the change will affect. People change roles, move companies, or retire, taking their expertise with them.

For a goodly percentage of systems in a large enterprise, it is probable that no one is available who understands what's going on.

Obviously, when changes are being considered in these circumstances, there is every possibility something unexpected will go wrong.

CIOs know this, so they insist on testing every change. But, once again, they are hamstrung by complexity.

To properly test a change, one needs an exact copy of the live system on which to do the test. Most organisations don't have multiple copies of their live systems, because the cost of providing them is too great. You'd have to duplicate every server, every piece of data, and all the programmes and processes to get certainty in such a situation. Generally, neither the time nor money is available to do that.

Thus, even small changes are risky propositions for CIOs. They try to mitigate the risks by doing work when processing loads are low, such as on weekends. They have multiple people on standby equipped with back-out plans, so if anything does go wrong, they have at least the capability to undo the change. And, of course, they rehearse their disaster scenarios in case the worst happens.

As you'd expect, this all costs money, and those costs quickly mount up. Add the fact there will likely be multiple changes scheduled in every single change window (i.e., a weekend), and you can see why modification to systems is so expensive and risky for CIOs.

If avoidance of unintended consequences is the first reason IT is so expensive, the next is trying to prepare for failures. Networks sometimes go dark without notice. Servers might wear out and die. Databases get corrupted. And any number of other things can happen, all of which bring IT to its knees.

To combat this, CIOs will relentlessly seek out and eliminate what they call "single points of failure", or, in other words, those parts of their systems which, were they to go down, would bring down everything else.

The usual remediation for a single point of failure is duplication. For example, there will be at least two sites on which IT assets are deployed, because one might be damaged by a disaster or lose power. Within each site, everything that's critical will be duplicated, down to a data level. And between the sites there will be multiple network links. It all has to be paid for, even when most of it isn't used.

Duplication adds complexity and with it risk, so CIOs do everything they can to eliminate any change they don't have to accept.

Once unnecessary activity is eliminated, CIOs will examine the changes they are *forced* to make. These include those required by legislation or regulators, as well as any demanded by business colleagues. There isn't much choice with respect to either: they're required if the organisation is to keep producing.

Almost all the remaining IT budget will be spent implementing these changes, and if there is anything left at the end, the final thing CIOs care about is investing to reduce the cost of their operations.

It is a rare IT group that is directly responsible for the outputs of an organisation in its own right. Consequently, IT is seen as an expense which needs to be reduced. Since it spends so much of the money - technology is often the biggest expense after people - it is highly visible in P&L. Fellow board members therefore put considerable pressure on CIOs to reduce their costs annually.

Finding new ways to reduce the cost of operations has led senior technology managers to outsourcing, to service reduction, and to any number of other measures that let them deliver "good enough" for the smallest amount of money.

"Good enough", unfortunately, is the present state of the art for large technology groups. Lacking the ability to invest (because of the cost reduction imperative), the least expensive option able to deliver the majority of the requirements is always selected.

Finally, if there is any money left over after these priorities are satisfied, CIOs will look for investments they might make which, in the medium term, have risk or cost benefits.

For innovators who rely on technology to implement their goals, the way large IT organisations are optimised to take out cost and eliminate change is, perhaps, the top reason for failure to create decent returns with the necessary speed.

Now, CIOs aren't stupid. They realise their response to these cost and change challenges takes them out of the strategic loop altogether. It makes them "order takers", subservient to their business colleagues. They are constantly conscious that order-taking does not reflect the strategic role information technology ought to take in most businesses these days.

One response is the establishment of a technology-specific innovation team, tasked with leading the search for strategic investments a CIO might make. The point of doing this, often, is not so much to find and deliver change, but to prove to board level colleagues CIOs deserves a seat at the top table.

In such innovation teams, the mandate is often finding new ways of helping the business through technology. Translated, this means innovators set out to create propositions which will then be put to business colleagues in the hope at least a few will be accepted.

This strategy, reasons the cash-strapped CIO, takes little money. All that's really required is a few good, creative people with an eye on the future.

As you'd anticipate, nothing much happens when CIOs adopt this approach, because business stakeholders care little about unformed technology *ideas*. What *does* matter to them is ideas which are appropriately backed up with the execution needed to turn them into something they can sell.

Of course execution, as we've seen in previous chapters, always costs money.

Since it takes money to turn ideas into something real, and since CIOs usually have very little to spare, a technology based innovation team is often unable to achieve very much. They are left looking for alternatives to enable them to justify their existence.

The most common alternative they come up with is the *gadget*. Gadgets have all the shiny newness that innovation people get excited about. Even more importantly though, gadgets are newness packaged up in a form easily acceptable to business colleagues without the need to pay for (or risk) very much change.

Gadgets are all very well, but usually they don't have strategic-level impacts. They may be interesting and novel, but really business critical applications of gadgets usually require large operational changes before they are of much value.

Perhaps the best example of the successful adoption of a gadget is the ubiquitous provision of ATM machines by banks today.

Ubiquitous today, perhaps, but when banks first considered self-service machines able to dispense cash to customers, they were woefully unprepared. They had to build networks and systems capable of running 24 hours a day. Manage distribution of cash to all the dispensers. Handle customer queries and complaints. And, above all, they had to deal with potential significant business model change, since till that point, all customer interaction was handled through the intermediary of an employee of the bank.

Usually, an external business consideration is the driver of demand for a new business gadget. For banks, it was customer demand for longer banking hours and self service that made the ATM a reality.

On the other hand, a gadget hardly ever drives business demand itself, and organisations will usually not modify big strategic priorities just because one exists.

Gadget provision is generally a failing strategy for technology team based innovators in the long term.

Innovation teams in technology organisations may have a particularly hard time of it, but as we discussed at the start of this chapter, *any* genuinely new idea is at risk from the prioritisation of the technology group.

Innovators have little choice in these situations but finding a way to manage this. There are basically two strategies available for doing so.

The first is elimination of the technology team from innovation projects altogether. This is not necessarily as drastic as it sounds, and certain kinds of innovation are well suited to this approach.

Most organisations can divide their systems into two categories: those which are mission-critical and everything else.

For systems in the "everything else" category, finding someone other than IT to build the technology parts of a project is usually simple. The Internet, especially, has made acquiring and using technology more of a procurement exercise than any great technical challenge.

This is particularly true if the innovation is completely unprecedented for an organisation, and therefore has few interfaces to systems already in use.

Even if the innovation is completely disconnected from existing systems, however, it is likely there will be three objections raised by technologists.

The first will be security. IT will want to know if the supplier can match them in the level of protection they offer. Security is one of the key arguments IT groups use to justify their existence, so they are highly motivated to ensure the barrier is as high as possible for any third party that might encroach on their turf.

Technologists will argue they're protecting the information assets of an organisation, of course, but a peripheral concern will be to ascertain if they have any grounds to block the innovation. Given the choice, IT people always prefer to do things in-house and security is a prime excuse to do so.

On the other hand, if the argument results in a re-prioritisation of internal demands enabling an innovation to proceed, the outcome is positive no matter the underlying motivation of the technologists.

The second objection from an internal IT group will concern reliability: will the supplier offer the same kind of uptime internal technologists provide? Here, the concern is reputational. Because internal systems are fiendishly complex, most technology organisations do not have particularly good credentials in this area. Their fear is any external service will make them look poorly, and business colleagues will get into the habit of bypassing them for new functions they need.

Again, this can be a motivation for the technology team to reorganise their priorities so they can take on the project.

The last objection from IT will concern scalability, really a question of capacity. Will the new service work properly when the full load of all prospective users is applied? Can it handle the temporary peaks in volumes which occur at specific times of the week? Is the service cost effective compared to what could be done internally?

Once again, the internal IT organisation is at risk of odious comparisons with external providers. We've already examined the reasons IT is so expensive in large organisations. Specialist providers do not have to deal with complexity and risk to the same degree in many cases, and their pricing tends to make internal IT organisations look expensive by comparison.

For all these reasons, an IT group confronted with external procurement may make a special effort to help innovators regardless of their other workloads.

So much for systems which aren't mission critical.

By far the majority of innovations with strategic impacts *will* touch mission critical systems. In these cases, it becomes difficult to justify the removal of IT altogether, for various good and proper reasons.

Mission critical systems are the heart of in-house IT organisation. They are also so important to business colleagues that even the *idea* of allowing third parties to touch them will be difficult to accept.

A business case suggesting elimination of IT from a core system change usually has to be pretty spectacular before it has much chance of succeeding. As a rule, there's probably little point in progressing with this approach at all given the hurdles involved.

This leads us to the second strategy innovators may pursue to adjust the priorities of the technologists, and that is *coopertition*. Coopertition occurs when innovators and technologists work together because a competitive dynamic is added to the mix.

Practically speaking, what does this mean?

Let us pretend, for a moment, the innovation team has dreamed up a new piece of functionality reliant on core systems to a significant degree. They decide – in the spirit of adjusting the priorities of the technologists – that duplication of the functionality outside the core system is the easiest way to progress.

By suggesting they add functionality to core systems by building add-ons outside the direct control of Information Technology, the innovation team is able to initiate a competitive response. Essentially, the innovators raise the spectre of a new IT group largely duplicative of the one that already exists.

Confronted with this possibility, information technologists are highly motivated to change their prioritisation. They will either help the innovators with the implementation of the relevant functions, or they'll implement what's needed themselves in order to avoid losing control of systems critical to their futures down the line.

The key to coopertition is finding a trigger point allowing Information Technology to contribute within the boundaries of their prioritisation framework, which simultaneously avoids alienating them altogether.

Hard though it may be to avoid, alienation of IT groups is an obviously bad outcome because internal teams will generally be much better at running core systems than anyone else. Their expertise is to be prized, rather than isolated.

Neither are technologists personally responsible for the prioritisation frameworks they operate within. If their behaviour appears anti-innovation, it is the result of demands their business colleagues put on them.

It is, after all, the business that beats up IT when systems fall over. And it is the business that demands year on year reductions in operating cost even when there is little fat left.

Usually, information technologists aren't deliberately obstructive, so helping them be more agile in the presence of innovation is very helpful to both them and the overall organisation. Clever innovation teams do this through application of influence, through coopertition, and by finding scenarios where they can do work themselves without disintermediating Information Technology to any significant degree.

Case Study

SOME INDUSTRIES ARE more dependent on Information Technology than others. Banking and Financial Services in general are amongst those reliant on technology to an especially high degree.

In a bank I worked with once, the rigor of the change process was such that important updates often had to be booked half a year or more in advance to get through the IT paperwork involved.

This was exacerbated by a chronic shortage of change slots: the only available times were out of hours on weekends and late at night.

So significant were the challenges involved in making business-critical change happen, the idea that a semi-optional innovation could get through the process was almost laughable.

Consequently, when the innovation team proposed a new payments system to implement key business capabilities in a potentially strategic scenario, they had little choice but to adopt a coopertition approach.

The innovators started by determining which parts of the core systems they could reasonably duplicate without adding inordinate costs to the overall project. With this information in hand, they approached IT to provide an overnight batch update to keep both the proposed duplicate and the core system up to date.

Since such a batch already existed to keep other core systems synchronised, it was very difficult for IT to refuse, even though architecturally duplication was hardly an ideal approach to take.

Next, the innovators implemented their new functionality using a third party vendor able to host the functionality outside the core assets of the institution.

Finally the system went live - not without a few problems of course - demonstrating the innovators were able to get new functionality out the door relatively quickly.

Scroll forward a few months, and the payments innovation was taking off in the market, swiftly becoming a high volume system mission critical in its own right. The technologists, who till this point had provided minimum support only, determined the system now needed to be brought in-house to "safeguard service".

They rearranged their priorities to bring the system in-house in less than six months. Conveniently, this approach satisfied the innovators, who had wanted the solution in-house in the first place as well as the technologists, who now felt they were doing good work by changing their priorities.

Coopertition works.

Rule 7: Answer the
3 Key Questions

NOW WE'VE EXAMINED the important things needed prior to commencement of an innovation effort, it is time to turn our attention to those activities necessary once ideas have started to arrive.

Most innovation programmes, unfortunately, fail very quickly. This usually happens because they lack structured mechanisms to turn ideas into actual products and services.

Whilst it may be fun to dream up interesting concepts on whiteboards, the real game is making new things happen. The processes of doing so are typically much more involved than the initial effort spent creating the idea in the first place.

In this section, we'll examine methods to transform an idea from an initial spark of creativity into a well constructed business case suitable for funding.

If you're fortunate enough to have a reasonable pipeline of ideas at this stage, it is likely you will already have come to an important conclusion: not all ideas are equally good. Despite this, you may also have found relatively poor ideas have proceeded anyway.

This is a fact of life for an innovator, and real skill in the role is demonstrated by correctly guessing which things to support in order to maximise the success rate given the time invested.

Luckily, though, it is not all that difficult to de-risk a new innovation without doing much work. Actually, all you really have to do is answer three questions: "Can we do this?", "Should we do this?", and "When?".

We have briefly examined these questioned earlier in this book. Now it is time to look at them much more closely: they will be central to the success of most innovation efforts.

The determination of the 'Can we?' question is mainly technical. Sometimes very good ideas with fantastic business cases arrive, but once the implementation details are worked out, prove to be impossible to progress. This is particularly true when genuinely new processes or technologies are involved.

Routinely, implementation challenges aren't technical: they are legal, operational, or the result of human factors. Whatever the issues involved, the point of the "Can we?" question is determining if there is any reasonable way to overcome the challenges involved in the project.

There are many ways to do this, including running experiments, often called prototypes or pilots.

Pilots are an important contributor to an innovation process because they provide early and cheap insight into what is likely to happen when an innovation makes it to the wild. Pilots let an organisation "suck it and see" before they take whatever-it-is to a broad base of customers, many of whom will be so valuable that risking their business with something untried seems reckless.

A pilot is not a technology experiment to see if people will "like" the product or service, however. Neither is it a proof-point that whatever-it-is can be made to work in the first place or a sales tool used to help win funding. Pilots, being relatively complete from an implementation perspective, are *much* too expensive to be used in such a fashion.

If experiments are needed, prototypes are a better solution.

Prototypes are small demonstrations of specific features or attributes of a to-be innovation, not completely finished products and services in their own right.

Prototypes are good for resolving technical and political ambiguity.

They may be small, hardly functional demonstrations of what something could look like if it were built. Or, they may be experiments showing how a process or technology can work in a new, novel way. Prototypes answer a single question in isolation and usually have little value beyond.

Prototypes are entirely throw-away since they don't do anything very useful other than illustrate one, specific point. They are one of the best ways to answer the "Can we?" question, because they are usually very inexpensive to make.

After the "Can we?" question has been answered satisfactorily, the next thing to resolve is whether an innovation makes economic sense. This is the essential point of the next key question, which is "Should we?".

Since the goal of an innovation effort is to make money, most innovations will have positive benefits if they are to get off the ground. These will not in every case be financial, because though the main part of 'Should we?' is a business case, there will be other considerations as well, especially when the idea is genuinely unprecedented.

Some innovations, for example, stretch the boundaries of what is tolerable for risk and security people. The 'Should we?' question, for them, is one of prudence and operational exposure. There will be similar considerations for a whole raft of non-core stakeholders: human resources, legal, and many others.

Though these ancillary considerations are important, the financial case for an innovation remains the most important component of any answer to the "Should we?" key question.

One of the best tools available to innovators in this respect is the "Cash Curve", a line illustrating the balance between benefits and cost over time.

Typically, a cash curve will dip into negative territory quickly when an innovation projects starts as money and effort is expended on development and implementation. Thereafter, the curve returns to positive territory when benefits start to be realised.

An ideal innovation dips shallowly below the line at the start, then recovering positively as quickly as possible. Such a profile depicts an innovation with relatively low risks, probably because it is incremental in nature.

On the other hand, a cash curve with a very deep dip at the beginning and slow recovery indicates an innovation with many more significant risks, quite often because it is radical. Not only are upfront investments likely significant, payback will take much longer to materialise.

Obviously, the longer a project takes to return to positive territory on the cash curve, the more difficult for an innovation team to take a risk on it.

The final question innovators must answer is 'When?'.

Now theoretically, this is the question requiring the most judgment of all three, because it seeks to understand the benefit of investing immediately compared to those of delay. Not all good ideas are best executed by rushing in. Indeed, "fast follower" is often a far better strategy, especially when a firm is risk averse or confronted with something *so* new the technological risks are too hard to mitigate.

The real question is determining whether there is enough competitive advantage available if a firm is first to market. Often there is, especially when a network externality is present.

A network externality arises whenever an innovation is worth more to adopters as more people start using it.

The telephone is a great example of this. The value of the phone is you can pick it up and talk to anyone else. In its early days, though, telephonic communication was severely limited. Not everyone had the device, so it was easier to send a letter.

The value of the phone (and now, of cell phones), is directly proportional to how many people you can contact with them.

In the presence of a network externality there are significant competitive advantages available for being first to market. In the case of the telephone, most countries experienced the same phenomenon: one large telephone operator wound up controlling practically every customer, as all the smaller operators either went out of business or were acquired by their larger competitors. The larger operators – often monopoly providers in the end - were the ones who moved aggressively to capture the largest possible customer base.

Most of the time, though, there are no network externalities present in innovations, so the question becomes how early, relative to competitors, it is sensible to launch an innovation.

The reason for caution is simple: the earlier you enter a market with something genuinely new, the more expensive your innovation will be to operate during its serviceable life.

The dynamics driving this are these: the more unique something is, the more technology, process, or people uniqueness is involved. Everything swiftly becomes bespoke, designed for and required by the innovation. There is little chance to learn from the mistakes of others, so development costs tend to be high. And, because everything is one-off, operating expenses have no chance to decrease through economies of scale.

By contrast, an organisation adopting the "fast follower" strategy is able to observe the lessons learned by everyone who has gone before. With sufficient time, it may even be possible to buy some of the processes and technologies needed on the open market. Eventually, the innovation will be copied enough that its price will reflect its increasing commoditisation.

In the meantime, though, the organisation who entered first is still maintaining their very high initial cost base. This translates into a significant competitive advantage for later entrants.

Even if the three key questions come out positively, there is one further determination it is sensible to make: how much effort is the innovation likely to take to get funded?

It is helpful to consider this analogously to the process of getting an object into orbit by rocket. You need a certain amount of fuel, proportionate to the size of the payload.

In this case, the idea is the payload we're trying to launch to orbit. Bigger ideas take more fuel and a bigger rocket.

Many ideas have sufficient fuel to carry them part of the way themselves. You know the type: concepts so exciting they get individuals enthusiastic enough to consider taking time away from their day jobs to work on them.

But even the best ideas lack *all* the fuel they need to make it. You have to help them along.

The thing is, the supply of fuel an innovation team has is finite, and once used, there is rarely more available.

I was put in mind of this recently when having a discussion with a colleague. He'd come up with a great concept around customer experience in payments and brought it to our innovation team.

I told him I thought his concept was amazing, and asked "how much time can you give to work on this?".

Unsurprisingly the response was "I don't have time to do that and my day job".

People generally don't, which is why there ought to be an innovation team in first place.

In this case, the idea had enough fuel of its own to get to the innovation team, but insufficient to go beyond it. Our decision was whether to fuel this idea up to make it fly or not.

Fuelling up ideas is the biggest – and most time consuming – part of the job of innovators.

Endless meetings. Lots of sales calls. So much influencing to get the necessary alignments and agreements to proceed. It takes a lot of personal energy to get things rolling.

Whilst getting concepts moving initially is difficult, innovation projects often get quickly to a point where they have a life of their own.

One team I worked in, for example, was investigating something in the digital services space for 6 months before we decided to – as we called it – drown the puppy.

Despite heroic effort, our team was never able to find a decent answer to the "Should we?" key question, because the technical considerations introduced too much risk. And we were never able work out any answer at all to "When?", since there was neither any way to predict what competitors would do, *or* come to a decent costs analysis with respect to investment.

The problem came when we tried to stop working on the idea. By that time we'd fuelled it up with so much energy that everyone around us were *horrified* we wanted to stop. They prevented us drowning-the-puppy.

Work continues on that particular online concept to this day, not going anywhere, but not quite dying either. It is a distraction for everyone.

The point at which teams have worked on a concept so long it can no longer be stopped is similar to that when a rocket achieves escape velocity. It is leaving your control, and there is nothing you can do once it does.

Getting to the escape velocity of an idea is something one absolutely needs when the concept is good enough. Determining it is "good enough" in advance is the challenging part that rigorously applying the key questions can help with.

Before we leave the discussion of the key questions, there is one final point to be made about the escape velocity of ideas and that is this: when you're trying to drive innovations to orbit, be certain what you are doing isn't going to break the second it leaves your control. You have no ability to bring it back for repairs, even if it goes widely off course.

A broken innovation will reflect on an innovation team over and over again. People will always hold it up as an example of a great concept that lacked execution.

Case Study

EARLIER IN THIS book I described a situation where my colleagues and I had the idea of scraping bank web sites to represent transactions in a single web page. Account aggregation, as this process is called, was introduced successfully and independently by Yodlee. Though we also had the idea, we'd failed to add any fuel to get our version moving.

After we saw the success of Yodlee, however, we were motivated to duplicate their functionality ourselves. We hadn't been courageous enough to try for first-mover advantage, but decided we *would* attempt fast-follower. After all, if Yodlee could make it work, surely we could too.

At the time, account aggregation was genuinely new, and there was much market speculation the technique would, eventually, lead customers to abandon their banks' web sites altogether.

From the customer's perspective, the value proposition was convenience: instead of visiting multiple bank websites, they could go to just one for all their details. This 'single customer view' we talked about was to be the next killer financial services application.

When we asked ourselves the 'Should we?' question, therefore, the answer was most definitely "yes!".

Although the service would ostensibly be free, even the most conservative projection of revenues arising from cross-selling opportunities made the new offering extremely attractive. Our dream was based on what we might be able to do with all that lovely customer data ready to be mined and exploited.

We were not so blind as to imagine things would be simple, though. A key concern was whether it was actually *sensible* to screen scrape the web sites of other banks. What if something went wrong?

To make account aggregation work, customers have to hand over their Internet banking user IDs and PIN numbers, which are used by automated agents to gather data. Nightmare scenarios, including wholesale theft of secret numbers and user IDs for other bank's customers were considered.

Here, too, the answer to the 'Should we?' question was a cautious "yes". We felt the benefits accruing from the service outweighed most of the potential risks. *Especially* if this was going to be the next killer financial services application.

With the answer to 'Should we?' determined, we proceeded to the second of our three questions.

Our examination of the "Can we?" question meant we had to determine whether screen scraping could actually be done from a technological perspective. Examples from Yodlee aside, we created our own experiments.

With these in hand, we concluded screen scraping was, indeed, viable. We also worked out how to create a secure 'PIN Vault' that would make it practically impossible for anyone to steal customer details. A myriad of other details were also resolved at a high level, giving us confidence we could, technologically, implement the service.

The real question, though, was not technical at all.

Everything depended on what the regulator might think of customers handing over their secret details to a third party.

At the time, banking terms and conditions at most Australian institutions specifically forbade customers disclosing their login details to anyone, even another bank.

The penalty for doing so was invariably the loss of any guarantees if anything went wrong. Would the regulator countenance our situation given the potential advantages to the customer if it all worked?

This led to tense moments and some nerve wracking meetings whilst we attempted to get a read on the stance the regulator would take. We knew if we guessed wrong we'd probably invest hugely in something that would never be allowed to see the light of day.

We guessed right. The regulator gave us a cautious "Yes", having come to the conclusion account aggregation provided sufficient customer benefits to make taking a few residual risks worthwhile.

We proceeded onward, imagining we had, indeed, found the killer application that would change the face of online financial services.

When we finally got to the 'When?' question, however, we made significant errors in judgment.

Convinced of the bank-side benefits of the technology, we just assumed customers would flood to the service, chasing convenience of access to everything from one place.

This was a fallacious assumption. Customers were far more concerned about their security than we'd expected. The additional convenience they achieved was more than outweighed by their fear something might go wrong.

Adoption was slow, and then trailed off to nothing. We'd allowed our own excitement for the service to overshadow the need to check with customers. We didn't do any detailed analysis of likely adoption behaviour of customers at all.

In hindsight, it was an obvious mistake. Customers were, after all, already getting convenience from their new Internet banking sites. Did they really need all that much more?

One year after the service launched it was cancelled. None of the benefits we'd promised materialised, largely because we were far too early with the innovation. We didn't understand the proposition customers *would* be interested in, and completely underestimated the time it would take for them to accept the idea of trusting a third party with their financial information.

It seemed clear that account aggregation was doomed. Even Yodlee, the market leader wasn't doing all that well.

It was not until 2007 that account aggregation returned in force, but this time in the shape of personal finance management web sites. Their unique selling proposition was not convenience (a franchise well and truly served by banks with online banking) but managing money better.

Today, most banks are either considering deployment of account aggregation, or have done so already. There are a range of third party sites independent of banks, that offer similar capabilities.

Account aggregation has arrived, and it *is* a killer application.

Rule 8: Drown the Puppy

DOING INNOVATION FOR a living gives you a thick skin because more often than not, some of your best work never sees the light of day.

Typically, between 80% and 90% of concepts firms try will fail, failure that's the result of many factors most of which can't be controlled by the innovation team directly.

Whilst the failure rate is very hard to change - even the best innovation teams in the world aren't all that much better at getting things out the door if they are brutally honest with themselves - predicting what is likely to fail isn't all that difficult.

Predicting failure is the best strategy available to increase returns on innovation investments. If an innovation team cancels questionable projects quickly, they reduce the load on other investments since the degree of success they must achieve to break-even is much reduced.

The process of killing projects early is one I've sometimes styled "drowning the puppy". Why a puppy, I hear you ask?

When you have a new idea, the more time you work on it, the more emotionally engaged you get. It is just the same as loving a puppy. As you spend more time with the baby animal, decision making gets wound up in feelings, rather than what is reasonable.

As with a puppy, when it comes time to kill a concept early, especially if it has been the subject of sustained effort, you are likely to experience discomfort, even grief.

The moment evidence begins to accumulate things may not work for a particular concept is the best time to drown-the-puppy. As we've noted, converting an idea into reality takes execution, and execution costs money.

The least sensible reason innovators spend money is an emotional investment in something that seemed good on the whiteboard, but is increasingly unfeasible.

What are the signs its time to start drowning puppies?

The first sign, obviously, is an idea isn't able to demonstrate satisfactory answers to the 3 Key Questions we examined in the last chapter.

Clearly if one isn't able to work out the technical means to make an innovation work, there is little point proceeding. Neither is there much point continuing if the money doesn't add up, or if you know competitors can copy everything immediately.

These signs may be obvious, but you'd be surprised to discover how many organisations fail to drown-the-puppy even when it is patently clear one or more of the 3 Key Questions hasn't worked out.

There is, however, another significant sign that puppy drowning should take place. That sign is a political one: where there isn't sufficient internal support to take a new idea forward.

Sometimes, you have a business case which is amazing, and you know technically things are easily managed. You've assessed the competition, and you feel there is little, if any, chance they'll be able to respond in a meaningful way. Even with all these positive things to say about the prospective innovation, you may find none of the important people who can make a funding decision will say "Yes!". They aren't interested, or at least, don't appear to be interested.

Usually, this will boil down to internal politics.

Invariably, there are more political issues to manage for a given innovation than people-bandwidth available to deal with them. This especially true for younger innovation efforts (which must operate with limited senior executive support whilst they get their first wins) and for very big, transformational innovations that touch significant parts of the business.

In these cases, managing the political dimension becomes a resource prioritisation exercise. You want to spend the limited time available for managing and influencing in such a way you optimise the chance a concept can get funded and see the light of day.

It is less difficult to do this than might be imagined, as there are generally authority asymmetries in most organisations.

Authority asymmetries arise in firms because the number of individuals authorised to say "No" to things is much greater than the number who can give approval. The nay-sayers are allowed to shut things down because the consequence of doing so is status quo: nothing changes from what is presently in place, and a future with uncertainty is more frightening than the present known absolutely.

On the other hand, there will be a very small group of people who are actually empowered to say "Yes". These individuals may not always be senior managers with appropriate authorisation to do things. Sometimes, people decide for themselves they can say "Yes" and manage resulting consequences appropriately. The maxim about asking for forgiveness, not permission, is a description of these individuals.

Mostly, those with authority to say "No" and those that can say "Yes" don't overlap all that much. This is the authority asymmetry I referred to earlier, and it provides the opportunity to manage the politics involved in innovation effectively.

For a given idea, there is practically no upside for innovators if they influence people who are authorised to say "No", especially for the earliest parts of the influencing cycle. The best outcome possible, in fact, is they *don't* say "No", an outcome providing little value to the innovation effort.

Influencing someone who can say "Yes", however, is quite a different proposition. Whilst there is still the risk of a "No", even an ambivalent response hasn't hurt the chance of getting something out the door. But an official "Yes" is the breath of life for an idea. For an innovator, this is a much superior value proposition.

Maximising the return on influence means using authority asymmetries to ensure the greatest amount of time is spent with people who have the power to say "Yes". Conversely, using authority asymmetries wisely means ensuring concepts are as under-the-radar as possible for those who can only say "No".

How do you identify the difference between the two groups? My experience suggests those individuals without direct association with the actual money in a particular business line will most likely be authorised only to say "No". They are the ones who should be kept out of the innovation cycle for as long as is practicable.

Conversely, there are usually paybacks from influencing money-attached stakeholders as early as practicable.

Assuming you are able to manage authority asymmetries correctly (and thereby avoided drowning-the-puppy at the behest of nay-sayers), there is a further political determination to be made.

For every innovation successfully introduced, there are both winners and losers. The winners are those whose personal interests in an organisation are furthered when the new thing comes along. They'll be getting some sort of advantage over their peers, and will therefore likely support the innovation.

Of course, such advantages usually result in disadvantaging others, who will naturally be extremely motivated to shut the innovation down.

The political determination involved is whether the internal group obtaining the advantages from an innovation are more powerful than those suffering the disadvantage. If this equation works out the wrong way, there are only three options available to innovators.

The first is drowning-the-puppy immediately. Most of the time, this will be the most sensible option to select. It results in the minimum amount of effort, and enables innovation teams to move to opportunities with lower risks of failure.

This may not always be in an organisation's best interest, of course. Innovators are responsible for the future welfare of their firms, so drowning-the-puppy every time it looks like powerful people disagree with progress has very significant long term consequences.

Nonetheless, despite future best interest, there is little point continuing a concept which has *no* chance of success as a result of political dimensions. It is a painful, though very necessary judgment call innovators will be called on to make often.

The second option available is transferring benefits arising from the innovation from the winners to the losers. There are a few mechanisms for doing this, including offering opportunities to participate in the value upside, sharing the glory, and making it look as if the idea came from the losers in the first place.

This strategy works best for innovations which are largely incremental. Radical innovations are usually so strongly biased towards winners that simple measures aren't available to redress the balance.

The final option available to innovators is dependent on how much influence the team themselves have. It may be they are in a sufficiently powerful position they can force an innovation through regardless of any opposition.

The thing about influence – especially the kind needed for innovators – is you either have it by virtue of your position (i.e. you are senior in your own right), or you have it because you are associated with someone else who has influence.

This, by the way, is the reason so many studies suggest successful innovators almost always have the ear of the Chief Executive, or someone directly reporting to him or her.

This leads to an important question for innovators, especially at the start. What strategy should they adopt to get access to enough influence to effectively execute their roles as change agents?

Let us assume momentarily there is little influence available directly as a result of the hierarchical position of the innovation team. Innovation may be considered important, but no-one at the top really cares enough to prioritise it over other things.

This scenario means the question really boils down to one thing: how can a new innovation team demonstrate to someone with influence they should be closely associated with him or her?

In my earlier book *Innovation and The Future-Proof Bank* I proposed a five stage capability model describing the process of acquiring influence for innovation teams. Let's examine this model next.

Firstly, innovators have to prove they can do something, anything. It doesn't matter what, even the smallest successful idea makes a difference. Avoid the temptation to take on big programmes since without influence, they will go nowhere. Instead, take on a few, small, visible things. Make them work, and the team can move to the next stage.

The second stage for innovators is building a network of interested people who care about doing things differently. With the visible wins achieved previously, talk to everyone, anyone that will listen in fact, about how innovation can make a difference. Find the people who will help in the mission to drive change. Offer them opportunities to participate. Recognise that one person – even a small number of people – is never going to scale. Innovators need to recruit believers.

The third stage, once innovators have recruited all these people to help with the innovation problem, is making sure of predictability. Innovators need to ensure they can make a return routinely on the money their organisation gives them for investment.

Returns need to be predictable so senior leaders can trust - if they decide to make a bet on innovation - they won't look stupid. More importantly, if the team is generating real returns, such leaders will be interested in keeping innovation close, simply because it is something with the potential to make them look good.

When this happens, innovators have achieved at least a modicum of influence.

The fourth stage is using the tools of innovation to start influencing strategy by helping senior leaders rehearse important future decisions that relate to innovations. What is the likely impact of the competitor's recent hit release? How can it be countered? What will happen if we don't respond at all?

You'd be amazed at the power of this, especially when management discover they're ready to deal with something unexpected. Prepare leaders with influence often enough, and innovators are inevitably invited into top table discussions to help future planning.

The fifth stage arrives when innovators have enough influence in their own right they're given permission to disrupt major business lines themselves.

Reaching this stage is the ultimate point of being an innovator in the first place. Whilst management may not realise it entirely, the long term role of an innovation team is saving a firm from itself. Any organisation will be disrupted by a competitor given enough time: the real role of innovators therefore, is to ensure such disruptions come firmly from within where they can be controlled and managed.

As you might expect from this description, the process of gaining influence is a long one. This is why, at least at the start, innovation teams are well advised to examine the political dimension of any potential innovation carefully. More often than not, they'll likely find that drowning-the-puppy and moving on is a more certain way to achieve results than commencing a battle which cannot be won.

Thus far, we've examined a few key reasons why puppy drowning - a key skill for any innovation team wanting predictability of returns - may be required even for projects that have spectacular business cases.

This leads us to an examination of the converse situation, where a particular concept may not appear like a good idea to start with yet seems to pick up steam by itself whether or not the innovation team attempts to drown it or not.

Last year, I spent quite a bit of time on the phone to a North American Credit Union getting material for a case study. I was speaking with them because they'd released a significant social media site, and I wanted to get background on why the idea arose and more importantly, how they got it out the door.

What I expected was a story about the travails and tribulations of a small group with a vision trying to make a figurative super tanker turn on a dime.

But that wasn't what happened. The idea for this particular social media site grew itself in a number of team meetings. Then, it practically walked out the door without much push at all. The team had to steer but there was no need to force the implementation.

When I looked at the situation in more detail what I was expecting to find was an "innovation culture", an organisation that let its people create and rewarded them for it.

But that wasn't the case. I found instead, the innovation was a once-off not repeated since. How could such a thing happen, I wondered?

What occurred was a perfect storm of factors. An alignment of political, economic, brand and community that came together at just the right time. Everyone just said "yes". That is a very unusual thing. Most of the time, you have to do lots of sales, lots of politics, and lots of numbers to get anywhere at all.

In short, most innovation requires you to push uphill, using authority asymmetries to optimise the return on influence.

The reality is perfect innovation storms of this kind occur quite often in organisations, though they may not always be simple to find. When they do show up, however, they are almost always the result of three factors.

The first factor is a dire need, a burning platform. There is something pressing that needs doing and existing solutions aren't a good fit.

The second factor is money, or more particularly, there is someone who has some and is ready to spend it. Usually, you also need this budget holder to be sufficiently senior that few consultations have to occur before the "go" button can be pressed.

The final factor is political: everyone acknowledges the need, and wants to do something about it. This recognition overrides whatever personal agendas exist which would normally prevent things moving forward.

Where you have an idea which sits in the middle of such a perfect storm, you have what I call an *autonomic* innovation. No matter what the innovation team does, good or bad, things are going to progress by themselves.

Day to day, a typical innovation team will spend much of its time creating one or more of the autonomic innovation factors from scratch. Much of this effort can be redundant, because perfect storms are frequent, as long as you can see them.

Teams with very high success rates more often than not, have learned the art of spotting an autonomic innovation early. They then concentrate their efforts and are able to drive much more innovation than otherwise. In contrast though, teams which spend their time building concepts from scratch are much worse off. They rarely, if every, go beyond the 10% success rate I mentioned at the start of this chapter.

There is one final point that must be made about drowning-the-puppy, and that is one comes eventually to a point where it is no longer possible to kill off a concept without very significant consequences for the innovation team.

In the previous chapter, I described this using an analogy of getting a rocket into orbit. An idea can reach escape velocity, and at that point, it is beyond the control of innovators no matter what they do.

That point, of course, is the one where senior stakeholders have signed up, funding is committed and real work has started. From this point onward, the role of the innovation team is not drowning the puppy, but doing everything possible to ensure it does *not* drown, no matter the circumstances. Failure to keep the puppy alive once senior stakeholders have committed funds, their reputations and, perhaps, their careers leads swiftly to innovation trauma, a subject we've examined already elsewhere.

What is the level of involvement an innovation team should have in the actual translation of an idea into something real? It is tempting, perhaps, to imagine they should stay in charge and see the project through to the end.

Doing so quickly bogs down the overall innovation effort in detail. Innovation teams, don't forget, are supposed to be running a portfolio of new ideas. They don't really have the luxury of spending their time on one thing only.

On the other hand, it presents unacceptable risks to allow concepts to go unsupervised entirely. The possibility of organisational innovation trauma is very real, and must be guarded against.

The fact is the work of an innovator is only partially done when a new concept is sold to an organisation, its funding won, and everyone is excited and agreeable about everything. The reason is what happens next is a process of dilution of the original concept, sometimes to the point where it doesn't make sense to continue development of the innovation.

Where does all this dilution come from?

New things require behavioural changes in adopters. Behavioural changes are like breaking habits: they require effort and discipline if they are to be ingrained in the common way of doing things.

People therefore reframe whatever is new in terms of the effect it will have on them personally. If it is perceived that lots of personal change will be required, they immediately take steps to minimise the effort involved.

For technologists, this manifests itself as "de-scoping effort", and "technical challenges". For business people, you see it in statements such as "we don't want customers doing that", or "My teams can't possibly spend their time using this!".

The necessary compromises which must be made to ensure progress of the innovation need to be carefully managed if the new concept is to actually *stay* as innovative as it appeared when it was first agreed.

Innovators, if they are to avoid innovation trauma, must reinforce the original intent constantly. It means they'll spend time convincing technology people when they say things are too hard (and if they really *are* too hard, making sure it is not technologists determining what compromises are acceptable). It means they'll have to convince business people that changing the habits of their operations staff and customers is worthwhile.

It also means they have to keep the excitement alive during the inevitable periods where groups begin to wonder if all the effort is really worth it. Innovation trauma occurs because people get bored just as often as it does because a concept bombed spectacularly.

What should now be obvious from this discussion is whilst-ever it is the innovation team working on a new idea, perhaps with a small group of trusted collaborators, drowning-the-puppy is the best tool an innovation team has to ensure predictability of returns.

Once the team has fuelled up the idea and won funding, though, this changes. Once a large team has formed and real investment has started, puppy drowning is likely to lead to innovation trauma. This is the time innovators become cheerleaders for their concept, an activity which doesn't stop until the innovation is no longer seen as innovative.

When the majority accepts a new idea as "the way we do things here" it is indicative new habits have formed. The innovation is safely embedded, and then, and only then, is it safe for innovators to down tools and move on.

Rule 9:
Share Everything

IT SEEMS COUNTERINTUITIVE, but innovators who talk about their work, share their knowledge, and network widely seem to be much more successful than those who don't.

Many people mistakenly think an innovation team's value comes from the products it creates: the unique ideas coupled with execution that translate into revenue or cost efficiencies.

Because these innovation outputs are valuable to firms, it seems obvious they should be protected, and organisations use patents, trade secrets, or copyrights to make sure these protections are robust.

These are signs a company is working in an industrial or knowledge economy paradigm. Innovation economy companies behave differently.

In an innovation economy company, what deserves protection is not the specific outputs of the innovation team, but the *capabilities* of the team itself. One hit product may be valuable, certainly, but the ability to create a string of such products: that is priceless.

This is a realisation lost on some people, especially senior leaders in industrial and knowledge economy organisations with generations of sales based on a few important products or services.

Their history of success with these important offers tells them future services and products are likely to be similarly valuable.

In such an organisation, what would you expect is the first position management takes when it is suggested sharing with competitors is a sensible strategy?

The likely response is a swift "Are you mad?" as leadership looks at you with that funny expression you ordinarily when you've done something not quite socially right.

Earlier in this book, we examined the case of Proctor and Gamble, who deliberately shared everything with everyone they could find and made windfall financial gains as a result. They adopted one of the mainstays of an innovation economy company: Open Innovation.

As we saw briefly before, Open Innovation suggests unused intellectual property serves your best economic interests if it is licensed to competitors who might make use of it, rather than lying around unused. Conversely if competitors have something of value available, Open Innovation suggests reaching some accommodation with them in order to unlock latent value.

Open Innovation exemplifies the fundamental difference between innovation economy companies and those they supersede: competitive advantage derives from how well you *use* know-how, not how much know-how you *have*.

The ability to use know-how well in a particular problem space is a hard to replicate capability requiring development, investment, and (more often than not) long and sustained effort. This is why it is a source of competitive advantage.

For companies who aren't quite embracing the innovation economy, however, attitudes are somewhat more medieval, bound up in a race to ensure as many industrial and knowledge age assets are as secure from theft as possible.

Such medieval attitudes in management are easy to identify.

One sign is constant vetting of external communications initiated by the innovation team, no matter how insignificant. Another is nervousness when innovators participate in conference programmes. Yet another is elimination of collaboration technologies, or a failure to provide them in the first place.

However, the most significant sign of all is outright panic when management realises innovators are using social media outside the boundaries of their organisations. Or, even worse, when they've chosen to collaborate with other firms or individuals without the permission of management.

External contact with third parties, even competitors, is only a threat when management believes such communication will reduce the competitive advantages available to them. They'll think this as long as they imagine value comes from protected assets, rather than the ability to *use* those assets.

Unfortunately, this creates a problem for innovators who realise it is only through sharing they can do really significant man-on-the-moon type projects.

Such projects are often too large for a single firm to tackle independently, even though creating a workable solution might have huge potential benefits. Time and time again, collaboration has shown its enormous value in overcoming the obstacles of big innovation.

For example, a single lab would never have been able to sequence the human genome: it took thousands of scientists working in concert across commercial and academic boundaries to crack the final code.

Boeing would not have been able to design and manufacture either its current generation 777 aeroplane, nor its next generation Dreamliner, if it had had to develop all the technology involved itself. It drew on the resources and know-how of hundreds of its partners instead, coming to an appropriate commercial agreement with each one.

The evolution of the free, open-source operating system Linux would not have reached its present enterprise-ready state had not large companies and individual software developers handed over their intellectual property to the community, in some cases building businesses, and others not.

For a team stuck in a knowledge or industrial economy firm however, reliance on trade-secrets and other protections makes each innovation group an island. It limits really big, really significant innovations to the largest players in a particular category, those who can afford to fund the work required.

By adopting collaboration as a key component of the innovation business model, however, the scale of innovation that may be attempted is effectively unlimited.

As we've seen, protections for know-how such as patents and trade secrets are less important in an innovation economy company, because it is the ability *use* those assets which creates value.

This, unfortunately, leads to difficulties defining the nature of "value".

In the past it was easy: value was measured as a function of the assets you controlled and the revenue generated with them. These days, where assets, particularly knowledge assets, are shared to get the best innovation outcomes, that measure is obsolete.

What is a reasonable measure of value in these circumstances?

The answer is innovations become valuable because potential customers have *declared* they are valuable. They do this by adopting the innovation, and for each new person that does so, the value of the innovation increases.

Earlier in this book, we examined the effect of network externalities on innovations. As you'll recall, a network externality is present in innovations which increase in value as the number of users increase. For example, the telephone is valuable because you can talk to a large number of people on it. It would be far less valuable if only a small number of people had telephones.

Successful innovations *all* have network externalities, because they are discussed by adopting customers. This is the word-of-mouth effect, and it creates inherent value in things, even though there may not be a moat around the trade secrets, or patents, or other know-how.

This should be self evident, but it is surprising how many traditionalist thinkers fail to recognise it. They believe a good idea has to be supported by something you can put a moat around. Otherwise, it's not a *commercial* idea.

Such people have not, apparently noticed Facebook or LinkedIn. Neither have much defensible intellectual property in them. They're just good websites.

Or Twitter, a site which has hardly anything unique in it at all. It is a service that lets you record 140 characters, after all. What do you need for that? A web server and a database?

Another example is clothing manufacturer Threadless, whose business is producing t-Shirts using designs open-sourced from users. They are doing a very brisk trade, as is MoonPig in the UK, who make greeting cards along similar lines. Both companies are valuable not because their products are unique, but because they have large customer bases which talk about them and *with* them, constantly.

These are all innovations which are quite easily replicable. It would be possible to build a Twitter-thing in about 2 days using MS Access. They are replicable, yet they are valuable.

A new concept doesn't need a lot of patentable and defensible know-how to be successful, it just needs customers.

Having a large number of customers has another benefit which further adds value to an innovation.

It is often the case that groups of like-minded customers who have previously adopted an innovation will rally together when, by chance, they find themselves with a new problem they can solve. If their new problem is in an aligned space to that already addressed by the innovation, such groups will often tweak what they have to make it perform in a way that provides a solution.

The value this generates is the result of opening an entirely new customer segment that can adopt the innovation.

Perhaps one of the best examples of this behaviour is the Hackintosh movement, a group of like-minded computer programmers who take Apple's operating system software and force it to work on hardware not manufactured by Apple

Hackintosh computers became especially popular when Apple failed to produce a Netbook style product. Netbooks are small, cheap systems, designed for high portability, long battery life, and online access.

Because of this gap in Apple's product line, Hackintosh computers based on netbooks running other software swiftly became available. Neither Apple, nor the manufacturers of these commodity netbooks had expected or designed for this, but it was done by customers anyway.

For both Apple and netbook makers, this was a new niche they'd previously not been able to access.

These days, of course, some of the demand for Hackintosh systems, at least at the netbook end of the market, is being addressed by the Apple iPad.

There are many cases of this going on in almost all markets and across all product categories.

For example, a group of flight-geeks are creating interesting products for themselves in the unmanned aerial vehicle space, previously the domain of the military-industrial complex.

UAV's as they are known, are expensive pieces of military hardware, often used in battle for tactical intelligence.

Chris Anderson, editor of Wired magazine, instigated the interest in this project a few years ago. He decided he'd like to build a Do-It-Yourself UAV, and started experimenting with a remote control airplane and a robot made out of Lego MindStorms. He published his day-to-day progress on a web site he set up for the purpose.

Chris captured the imagination of like-minded individuals, and a group formed to make autopilots out of mobile phones, aerodynamic components out of model planes, and control software using open source code designed for other applications.

Today, the group sells open source autopilots with specific capabilities for UAVs, and the functionality of their creations – all based on products never intended to be used in pseudo-military UAV applications – is astounding.

Modifying products for one purpose in order to serve another is not a new phenomenon. Kids have been modding their cars, their game consoles, and every other sort of consumer device for years.

The thing is though, that much of the time to this point companies have been trying to make sure their products are *not* composed into other things without their permission.

Apple, for example, apparently had a behind-the-scenes fight with Dell to discontinue their Mini-9 netbook. It was, I'm told, too easy to turn into a Hackintosh. Apple have now specifically removed the software features that make it possible to create Hackintosh machines which run on Netbooks in the latest versions of their operating system.

Apple is famous for wanting to control every aspect of their product and customer experience. But this particular move runs in the face of a major change that's coming: the empowered customer who wants to co-innovate.

Co-innovation requires sharing and opening everything an organisation produces. It is another ramification of the decreasing importance of intellectual property protection: much more value is available if customers are simply able to do what they want with whatever a firm creates.

So far, in this chapter, we've discussed the significant advantages which accrue to organisations who decide to share everything. Naturally, there are situations when it is not always appropriate to share, though these tend to be relatively few. Almost always, the decision not to share know-how is mandated by internal factors – often political - rather than concern about loss of value.

When such factors arise, running an innovation under-the-radar is appropriate.

The term "under-the-radar" has all these stealth connotations, as if an innovation team is doing something it shouldn't. This is not an accurate characterisation of the situation, however.

For a decent success rate, innovators necessarily have to manage so many stakeholders that applying some methodology to what they tell people is pretty much a given. It is necessary to be mindful that not everyone can know everything all the time.

What are the main reasons it might be necessary to avoid sharing everything and to run under-the-radar?

The first is the innovation team is faced with a mother-ship problem. Such problems occur when a powerful and successful business line is touched by a disruptive innovation which might interfere with revenues at some time in the future.

P&L owners of such business lines fight tooth and nail against the introduction of the innovation knowing it will cannibalise their revenues. They know their futures are in jeopardy if they fail to defeat it, so they are highly motivated to do whatever it takes to ensure their own positions are secure.

No matter what P&L owners might think about it, a disruption to core business operations by an internal innovation team is often far preferable to one which comes from outside.

Paypal's disruptive entry to the payments business of banks is an example of this.

Bankers, when they first became aware of PayPal, could not have imagined it would grow into the largest institution (by number of accounts) in the world. Even if they *had* correctly guessed at what PayPal might become, they would certainly never have mandated anyone doing much to counter the threat. Building an internal PayPal would have been seen as disruptive to existing payments businesses, and line of business managers, typically, are concerned with preserving what is working now.

The opportunity of response has now been missed, of course. There are few ways for bankers to respond to the near-monopoly PayPal has over the online payments market short of an expensive, all-out global assault. It is extremely difficult to imagine, given the low margin business that PayPal now dominates, how an incumbent bank could construct a business case to allow them to sustain a long term war of attrition. It is entirely possible banks have lost their position in online payments forever.

The only way any bank was going to create an effective competitive response to PayPal early enough was if its innovation team had hidden their activities from core payment businesses until it became obvious their work was necessary to long term survival.

Under-the-radar is appropriate whenever it seems obvious the mother ship business is likely to kill anything which interferes with its future, even when its future is under threat anyway.

The second reason it may make sense to work under-the-radar is when the team is moving resources into an area over which no organisational line presently has purview. When they enter a new area, especially one without revenues at the start, they always get push-back from decision makers who don't see any value in it for them.

In this case, the worst thing possible is the innovation is considered immaterial to the main business and shut down. The second worst thing is it is considered irrelevant and ignored. Teams facing such circumstances have to be under-the-radar until they have something sufficiently well-formed it's obvious to everyone that value has been created.

A third reason for under-the-radar is when it becomes clear existing business lines don't like (or refuse to embrace) change.

Change is painful and disruptive. The transformational part of change usually happens some time after the pain part. It is easy for stakeholders to focus on the pain, but being under-the-radar means the innovation team can hide at least some of it until the transformation potential becomes obvious.

The fourth reason an innovation team may choose to operate under-the-radar is when it becomes clear there are political sensitivities involved.

Often, an innovation will stomp directly on someone else's agenda. Since it is inevitable this will occur eventually the key questions to resolve are twofold: does the innovation team or its sponsor have the political capital to continue, and, even if they do is it better to steer clear of the whole area anyway?

Being under-the-radar means these decisions can be delayed until enough information has been collected to answer both questions.

It will almost certainly be a good idea, at least initially, to run under-the-radar when an innovation is outlandish compared to what is already being done. Faced with something truly unprecedented, conservative minds will always see the part which is immediately disruptive, but may not be so clear with respect to the end-goal.

The conservative minds are steady managers with successes under their belts, so they *think* they know what's best. It is unlikely innovators will have much of an opportunity to change their views unless they are able to *demonstrate* why their ideas are valuable.

Operating under-the-radar until such a demonstration is possible is one way to handle conservative, steady managers who believe they know best.

The final reason under-the-radar make sense is the team has no money. In this case, you are under-the-radar by necessity. You're doing everything with cast off parts and bits of string. You are under-the-radar because you don't have enough cash to force yourself above it. You hope your bits of string and cast off parts will eventually be interesting enough someone will take notice and help you move things forward. But in the meantime, being under-the-radar means you have to do a lot more work than you otherwise would.

Case Study

WHAT IS THE result of failing to share innovative ideas and concepts? In the case of the steam engine, James Watt, the noted inventor credited with the first really workable machines, spent a significant percentage of his time trying to derail the creativity of other inventors through his control of key patents.

It has been argued by some commentators that this was the principal reason the start of the industrial revolution was delayed by 30 years longer than it ought to have been.

Early steam engines were not very efficient. In fact, the first engines, used in mines to pump out water, were so inefficient their application was possible only in very shallow shafts convenient to a ready supply of coal.

In order to raise water any distance multiple steam engines, working together at different levels of the mine were needed. In most cases, it was cheaper to use animal or human labour than pay for the fuel.

When James Watt finally innovated to create a slightly more efficient engine useable in more difficult economic situations, his immediate first action was securing patent control over his invention, control he defended rigorously via the legal system for the next 30 years.

Watt's business model was based on the practice of licensing key inventions needed to make steam engines. Anyone could build an engine, but they had to pay Watt a royalty on each.

As a result few steam engines were built during the period of his monopoly because of cost. Growth in the technology was slow: year on year, during this period, the United Kingdom added about 750 horsepower of capacity a year.

In the years following the expiration of Watt's patents, however, capacity increased by 4000 horsepower a year and engine efficiency increased almost fivefold a year as well.

Applications of steam power started to spread quickly, and with freedom to innovate, many hundreds of creative minds proposed and implemented improvements.

The steam engine proved, subsequently, to be one of the most important technologies of all time, driving innovations in transport, production, machining, and almost every other area of human endeavour. The world changed radically, and the standard of living for those in industrialising countries rose quickly.

That these gains were delayed nearly three decades because of patent control is illustrative of the significant downside that exists when organisations seek to limit the spread of their intellectual property.

From the point of view of Watt, of course, seeking to maximise individual returns in a framework of industrial economics was entirely rational behaviour. What was rational then is not necessarily rational in today's competitive market, however.

What is happening now is even companies which have traditionally based themselves in industrial age economic frameworks are waking up to the power of sharing their intellectual property.

One such company is Vancouver based GoldCorp. GoldCorp is a mining company which, today, is the lowest cost, fastest growing senior gold producer in the world. It employs 10,000 people, and has mines in politically low-risk countries throughout the Americas.

It also has superb geological data.

Geological data is the key asset of any mineral exploration company, and the intellectual property involved in its creation and analysis are expensive and carefully guarded secrets.

When GoldCorp's CEO, Rob McEwen took the helm, he did something no other mining company executive had ever done. He released the company's crown jewels - all this highly valuable geophysical data - and offered a cash prize to anyone who could help him and his company find gold.

More than 1000 people participated in the challenge, a massive increase in prospecting capacity considering the limited resources GoldCorp was able to maintain internally.

The competition resulted in identification of 110 mining targets, and 80% of these led to new gold deposits.

In pure economic terms, GoldGorp has now developed more than 8 million ounces of gold using this process, representing an unbelievable return on its prize money offering - a minuscule $575,000 US dollars.

Rule 10:
Manage the People

THE LAST RULE for those starting an innovation effort concerns people. It is people, after all, who come up with the ideas. It is people who have the skills and experience needed to convert them into real products and services. In the end, it is also people who have to choose to use the innovations created by firms.

Earlier, we examined the capabilities required in an innovation leader. Now it is time to examine the necessary characteristics of people who will actually be creating innovations themselves. These include individuals both inside and outside an innovation team.

There are really two dimensions to consider here. The first (and probably most important) is whether for a particular innovation, you have the right mix of individuals in the team to drive a successful outcome. As we'll see in a moment, an improperly constituted innovation team always results in very little innovation getting done.

The second dimension to consider is the age of the innovation team. We'll examine this dimension first.

In most workplaces, there are three generations of workers. Now before I proceed to describe the three, I'd like to preface what follows with a note that these are generalisations of types, and don't always apply to every single person in every single generation. I have been criticised on more than one occasion for seeming ageism. It is not intentional or malicious, I assure you.

Having said that, the first group we'll consider are the Traditionalists, those who were born some time before 1965. At this stage in their careers they are often extremely influential in their organisations, and even if they're not in charge they will be close to the individual who is.

They're called the Traditionalists though, because they're the ones who embody the values one is most likely to see amongst the "old school". They will, for example, prefer to communicate through rigid and structured hierarchies and will certainly be command-and-control oriented in the way they distribute work between themselves.

When they need to make decisions, they will do so only so far as their perception of their personal authority level allows them and thereafter they'll seek direction from more senior individuals before they'll proceed with anything.

As innovators, this group will normally prefer to solve problems they've been directed to examine and will usually come up with solutions along trajectories which are well established by their organisations. This, naturally, makes them ideally suited to innovation teams who have elected to follow a Play-Not-2-Lose strategy and whose primary focus is on incremental innovation.

The second generation in most workforces is known as "X" and includes individuals who were born roughly between 1965 and 1983. In contrast to traditionalists, who will likely have worked in their present organisations almost all their careers, X-ers will have moved around quite a bit in the process developing broad experience in a range of scenarios.

X-ers can operate in a command-and-control environment, but prefer a much more flexible working style. They believe employees are powerful forces (both individually and in groups) and should be given a degree of liberty in the kinds of challenges and problems they'll solve.

When X-ers lead teams, they tend to act as coaches rather than authoritarian dictators and expect their teams to be participative in substantive decisions. They are inclusive and are more likely to give a pep-talk than a reprimand.

When faced with an innovation challenge, X-ers will generally proceed to examination of similar situations in other industries looking for solutions they can bring back to their own organisations. Theirs is the catch-cry "where have you done this before?" so hated by vendors trying to sell genuine innovation which hasn't ever been implemented previously.

They'll excel in innovation environments where either Play-2-Win or Play-Not-2-Lose is the strategy though they are usually not that interested in incremental innovation. Incremental innovation doesn't offer much in the way of opportunity for them to showcase the broadness of their experience and thinking.

For X-ers, what they know *and* where they learnt it is the factor that drives status in organisations. That's in contrast to Traditionalists where status is a consequence of tenure.

The final generation we'll consider are the "Y-ers". Generation-Y was born any time after 1984 and has a quite different approach to the workplace than either of the generations which preceded it.

Firstly, this is a generation which grew up with digital tools and online collaboration and they find such tools indispensable. This is in stark contrast to Generation-X, who probably learned how to use technology in the workplace, and the Traditionalists who may not have learned technology at all.

Generation-Y cares little about hierarchy or command-and-control. They team naturally and the leadership role switches amongst them naturally depending on the task at hand.

Their digital connection gives them very broad reach to global thinking and insight, and they will often know much more about the workings of the world outside their organisations than either of the two previous generations.

This broad grasp of the world makes a Generation-Y innovator very effective when a particular innovation problem needs a radical solution.

Broadness of thinking lends itself to out-of-the-box ideas and since Y-ers are unconstrained by conventional ways of doing things they will often pursue opportunities that X-ers will write off as "too risky" and Traditionalists as "impossible".

On the other hand, a Generation-Y innovator will usually not be particularly interested in incremental innovation and when they are forced into it, may dream up a radical approach just to keep themselves interested.

Though they are equally at home in Play-2-Win and Play-Not-2-Lose environments their preference is the former. Being relatively young in comparison to colleagues, they are idealistic and want to change the world not prop it up whilst it limps along the same course it has always done.

As I mentioned this categorisation is stereo-typical, and it is clearly possible for traditionalists to create radical innovation and for Generation-Y to do incremental. However, my experience suggests this is a categorisation that is as good as any when you want to take the risk out of an innovation effort

There is, however, one factor which can make all generations equally able no matter the type of innovation desired: the degree to which the innovators broaden their interpersonal and knowledge networks with other leading thinkers and innovators.

Usually, this is happens through digital means, but whether digital media is involved or not there is a stark difference between the performance of innovators with connections and those that without.

The connected always have a good grasp of the latest trends, the most recent thinking, and the breakthrough work going on in their specific area. They are always current because they have built networks of like-minded people with whom they are constantly in touch. This network acts like a big net, filtering an ocean of data and providing them with highly targeted, relevant items for absorption.

Maintaining such a network is a big time commitment, because you have to contribute to the network as well as suck from it. Then too, there is the initial effort of building the network in the first place, and the time spent keeping it active after.

For innovators, this tends to manifest itself in constant communication (probably on multiple devices), membership in multiple social networks, and never-ending content-creation using, for example, blogs and Twitter.

When you work with the connected in your particular interest area there is almost never any need to explain fundamentals, and it's reasonable to assume everyone will know everything that's current at present. Consequently, discussion immediately moves to applications, to what can be done with the current state of the art. The connected, it has been said, are able to give themselves PhD level educations in the things they're interested in, courtesy of Google and the Internet.

When dealing with the connected things happen more quickly. They need to, because with all that connection going on the pace of change is fast, fast, fast.

By contrast, the performance of innovators who *don't* build big networks is usually lack-lustre. Such individuals tend to be locked firmly in the dark ages of tour-guided information consumption. They digest analyst reports, use Google to read what companies and (sometimes) other thought leaders have said and based on this, will likely rephrase some amalgamated view of the current state of play.

You almost never get originality from those without connections. They don't have time you see, to be up to date enough to be original.

Now, of course, there is a finite upper limit to how much of this connecting stuff one can do before there is no time for anything else, such as the actual tasks involved in innovation.

The frustrating thing though, is dealing with innovation people whose jobs it is to know the current state of play, but fail to invest some of their time in understanding current state of the art. It is these types of course, who fail to defy the broad stereotypes with which I opened this chapter.

So, the first dimension to consider when structuring an innovation team or even when choosing a group to work on a specific innovation, is which generation of the work-force is likely to be most successful. It follows that, for a balanced innovation team, you really want to ensure you have a diverse set of people from each generation to make sure you can optimise your chances of success.

The other dimension one needs to consider is the individual innovation preferences of each person you're thinking about including.

Everyone is different and this is true even so far as how individuals approach the innovation challenge. There are at four major preference groupings, and most innovators align themselves to one or at most two.

The first innovation preference is the *Innovator-Creator*. We all know these kinds of people – they're the ones who come up with a constant stream of new ideas. Their great talent is finding inspiration in their surroundings and using it to create uniqueness. Innovator-Creators, quite literally, see money growing on trees.

The Innovator-Creator is very exciting to be around because they're always upbeat, positive, and come up with that out-of-the-box thinking that challenges everyone around them.

However, the work they do can be extremely distracting.

The problem is Innovator-Creators get bored quickly. Sometimes, when they're halfway through a work item, even if they've invested weeks, they may just drop tools and start a "better way of doing things" rather than finish what is already in train.

This is the major flaw of the Innovator-Creator: they are usually extremely poor at implementation. They may be great at thinking new things up, but asking them to finish what they've started almost always ends up in tears.

This is true even if they are given resources sufficient to allow delegation of all the operational aspects of what they set out to achieve. They are characterised by very short attention spans so they'd much rather be dreaming up something new to do than completing what they've already committed to.

Innovator-Creators are also rather poor at seeing the downside of the ideas they've created. Because they find the process of creating things so exciting (even to the extent, sometimes, of behaving as if they are addicted to the high creation gives them) they don't take note of anything making their new magnum-opus appear less than perfect. The result is they'll often start work on concepts which are really, truly stupid, only to have them blow up in their faces later on.

This is why you simply must have at least one innovator in the next category if you want to avoid massive, embarrassing failures of the sort that lead to innovation trauma.

That next category is the *Innovator-Embellisher*, an innovation preference that's about taking ideas which already exist and refining them to fit an appropriate local context.

If the Innovator-Creator sees money growing on trees, it is the Embellisher who will notice the tree is standing in a firm's garden and can therefore be harvested.

The real role of the Innovator-Embellisher is taking an idea from the Creators and contextualising it so it makes sense in a business context relevant to the firm. Their talent is being able to communicate the specifics of an idea in a way that allows everyone else to understand why it matters. They are great at stirring up excitement and they're superlative salespeople of the "vision".

You need an Embellisher around if you want an idea to get beyond the whiteboard stage because they're the people who know how to create enough impetus to get the real ball rolling.

That's not to say Innovator-Embellishers don't have a few faults of their own. Chief amongst these are the lack of grounding in the realities of do-ability. The three Key Questions which we covered in some detail earlier in this book, aren't something the Embellisher will bother with much.

The answer to "Should we?" is always "Of course we should!". When asked "When?", the answer is always "Right now!", and the "Can we do it?" question has the predictable response "Anything is possible!".

Innovator-Embellishers may be about creating excitement, but they are certainly not the sort of innovator you need if you want to get things implemented. You want them around to get enough buy-in from stakeholders to get things started but once you have, it becomes necessary to get an innovator with the next preference involved.

That preference is the *Innovator-Perfector*.

By contrast with the two preferences we've seen thus far, the Perfector is interested in analysing an idea to find its flaws. By doing so, he or she will seek to eliminate those ideas which (no matter how exciting and popular) are unlikely to be practicable once implementation starts.

The Perfector's credo is the three Key Questions, and he or she is expert at getting the correct answers and drowning-the-puppy if they're not favourable.

It is always left to the Innovator-Perfector to determine why something can't be done and to shut down an idea before innovation trauma becomes a real possibility.

Of course, the Perfector has some drawbacks as well. The primary one is he or she will, left unchecked, tip the balance of do-ability versus risk so far towards the former that breakthrough, radical innovations are never attempted at all.

By always needing to know in advance the steps required to achieve something, any innovation with significant degrees of uncertainty will almost always get puppy-drowned. The result is that Perfectors, left to their own devices, would allows only incremental innovation *regardless* of the potential upside.

In the early days of an innovation effort of course, this is probably not a bad thing because getting the early wins is best done with the minimum uncertainty possible.

Later on though, such risk aversion can be a significant liability because teams have to create ground-breaking newness in order to justify their existence. This is where the Embellisher is a natural counter to the Perfector - the two balance each other out.

The final innovation preference is the *Innovator-Implementer*. These are those unique individuals who can take what is mostly conceptual and turn it into a plan of action. They are the people who know how to refine an idea that's been analysed (and agreed) by Perfectors and turn it into a real project with a chance of succeeding. Once they've done that, Implementers are the ones who ensure the plan is followed to the end.

Of all the innovation preferences, the Implementer is the least understood. They rarely come up with truly new ideas, and neither are they very good at spotting opportunities which the ideas enable. Implementers also relatively poor at generating the excitement that's needed to cause stakeholders to buy into whatever-it-is in the first place.

These characteristics make it look like Implementers lack the special skills needed to be part of an innovation effort. It is easy to mistake their inherent focus on delivery for disinterest in doing things which are genuinely new.

The point must be made, however, that all the other innovation preferences are wasted unless you have a decent Implementer on a team. They are, after all, the only ones who have what it takes to turn ideas into something real. They are the *doers*, and all the other preferences are *talkers*.

It takes a very special kind of person to see through the uncertainty of an endeavour that's never been done before and turn it into a set of steps resulting in a new product or service.

Implementers are the rarest of the innovation preferences because though they may seem like process-centric project managers, they are really unique individuals with a combination of high personal innovativeness, attention to detail even when surrounded by incredibly distracting blue-sky thinking and extreme stamina and discipline. These are characteristics which allow them to get on with the task of execution whilst everyone around them moves on to things more interesting.

Most innovation efforts fail if there isn't an Implementer on the team. Unfortunately though, the other innovation preferences tend not to value implementation and execution as highly they ought to, and will therefore often hire other innovators in their own image. When this happens nothing gets done, the money isn't created from new ideas, and the innovation effort is generally cancelled in 18 months or less.

Teams without Implementers have fallen foul of a common misbelief: a good idea not only sells itself, it is capable of *building* itself as well.

Now, practically speaking, no individual will have only a one innovation preference. Most people have a mix of at least two, though they tend to cluster around either Creator-Embellishers or Perfector-Implementers. It's easy to see why: the former is about the blue-sky big picture stuff, while the later is detail and outcome oriented.

This leads to a very important conclusion: for any given innovation effort, the minimum number of people needed is two, each having at least two of the innovation preferences. Structured assessment of any potential innovator is advisable before kicking off a project if you want to minimise the chance your innovation effort will go off the rails.

Before we leave the people part of this book, we now turn our attention finally, to the subject of the customers that will actually use the innovation.

As I've mentioned elsewhere, actually adopting an innovation is akin to breaking a habit – it takes effort and personal commitment to do so. Most people can't be bothered if what they have is presently good enough and meets most of their needs.

There is, however, a group of people who don't display this characteristic. Instead, they actively seek uncertainty and newness and are actually turned on by it. They'll always be the ones who have the latest gadget and who love to experiment.

Demographically, these are individuals who tend to have superior access to financial resources, so it doesn't matter if things don't work perfectly. They are well educated and their broad interest in things beyond their present experience sets them apart from peers. In any given audience for a product or service, this group represents about 2.5% of the total on average.

This is an especially important demographic for an innovation team because it is the only group that will be bothered to try anything genuinely, actually new. Everyone else needs positive reinforcement by word-of-mouth from trusted associates before they'll bother with the effort it takes to adopt.

How do you know you're talking to someone in this group? Check the devices they use and the things they read. How many social networks are they part of and what do they talk about when you ask them questions? If the answers to all these things are bleeding edge, you have your answer.

From an adoption perspective, these are the most important individuals in any market. When an innovation is first launched, they are the only people available with the requisite risk appetite to try something new without hearing positive messages from people they trust.

Once it is accepted only 2.5% of a market will ever adopt something innovative without positive reinforcement from other sources, one comes to a realisation that changes the launch paradigm for everything: mass media marketing for innovation is a huge waste of money. By targeting the whole market you waste resources by shot-gunning messages to everyone when only a tiny segment has any inclination to listen.

It is far better to seek out that small 2.5% segment who are able to adopt immediately. If they like the innovation, its success, whilst not certain, is much more likely. These first adopters will tell their friends, family and acquaintances about their experiences, who may then adopt on the strength of their advice.

You may be interested to know that only a further 13.5% of the market will actually listen to the initial adopters we've been describing so far. They have a level of risk aversion which is high enough to prevent them trying something in the absence of any positive messages from trusted associates, but they don't need to see *everyone* using the innovation before they're willing to give it a go.

This second group, which innovation theorists term "early adopters", is important because not only are they happy to try new things with a minimum of positive reinforcement, they are close enough to the demographic of the rest of the market that they're acceptable referees for everyone else. Once you have penetration in the Early Adopter category the long term success of your innovation is assured.

The way new innovations are adopted in populations is a fascinating topic and is the subject of an entire science called Innovation Diffusion. For more information, I recommend a search on Wikipedia, which has excellent pages on this topic.

Case Study

ON ONE OF my trips overseas to visit bank innovation programmes, I had the chance to meet two different teams in institutions in South America. One was extremely successful with a steady portfolio of new ideas creating a decent return every year.

They were a team that seemed to have cracked the Innovation Management code: they knew how to turn various good ideas they were getting from customers and employees into process improvements, services and products. They had a success rate of about 11%, which is rather good. That translated into about 30 new introductions a year.

The other team was from a much larger institution and was much better funded. They had similar processes and systems in place for managing the innovation pipeline and they, too, were getting very good ideas from customers and employees. Their success rate, though, was somewhere less than 1%, and (though they wouldn't tell me directly) it may have been close to zero.

The interesting thing about these two institutions is they had similar innovation environments, even (allowing for scale) quite similar idea flow, but such drastically different success rates. Apparently, for the poorly performing team, even throwing money at the problem wasn't helping.

I had the chance to analyse this (actually, I was visiting because of a cry for help from the poorly performing team). And what I found wasn't surprising.

The poorly performing team was comprised entirely of Creator-Embellishers. Their leader, a Creator-Embellisher himself, had chosen people he liked and got along with rather than taking care to choose people who would minimise the chance of failure.

It is an understandable error: blue-sky thinkers who love new and interesting ideas often find themselves impatient with the more dogmatic nature of the Perfector-Implementers.

The composition of the poorly performing team explains the superior access to funding it had. Comprised entirely of individuals whose core talent was dreaming up great ideas and getting everyone else excited about them, it is hardly surprising they had more money.

It is easy to get money when there is an air of excitement around. It is hard to keep it though, when nothing substantive happens.

My examination of the successful team was also unsurprising. They were well balanced, with a decent number of Perfector-Implementers. If anything, they had rather more of them than they really needed. No-one thought the team was doing especially exciting work and in fact, innovation was seen as just another business-as-usual activity.

Getting money for each project was a big effort for this team, but every time they actually won money they made sure their ideas turned into something real. They may not have been exciting, but they were reliable. The team was building a reputation from the ground up in a sustainable, long term way.

The poorly performing team of course, had nothing at all long term about them. Recently, in fact, I heard their innovation effort had been shut down. The only surprising thing to me was that this took almost three years rather than the more typical year and a half.

Conclusion

IF YOU'VE READ this far, you now know enough to (at least) start your innovation effort in a way likely to bring success. The question you must now be asking having digested this book, is what you should do next?

It is a very good question. The answer is simple: just start innovating.

As I mentioned in the introduction there is no single text you'll be able to find that will tell you how to run an innovation effort that works in your *specific* organisation. Building an innovation capability takes time, and it takes practical experience which is earned through doing.

Every innovation effort is different. Just starting is the only way to build the skills which will lead to sustainable success.

Having said that, there are theoretical tools which will be useful in guiding the overall shape of your programme.

Firstly, if you have the time, I recommend you read E.M. Rogers' *The Diffusion of Innovation*.

Rogers was the founding thinker who first noted new ideas are spread through populations in particular ways. He posited the two stage adoption model now enshrined in "word-of-mouth" marketing: the idea people will tell each other about things they like, and this will make it more likely that those they tell will also adopt. He was also the initiator of the idea of "early adopters", "laggards" and so forth.

The Diffusion of Innovations is a big, thick text, but well worth the read if you want the broadest possible understanding of the mechanics of innovation science.

The next book you should consider is Clayton Christensen's *The Innovator's Dilemma*. After Rogers, Christensen is possibly the most influential innovation thinker of modern times. He's the man who first provided a theoretical construction to explain the way established companies and products are overturned by new entrants, who on the face of it, have no chance at all of succeeding.

Finally, there are hundreds of other books on practical innovation topics. If there is a specific tome on innovation management for your industry I suggest you read that too. I, for example, wrote *Innovation and the Future-Proof Bank* which explains how to do innovation management for bankers. There are similar texts for almost every other industry.

I'd try to avoid the non-industry specific texts, though. They tend to be full of high level advice without much practical application.

Next, having gotten through the activities recommended in the 10 rules in this book there are a couple of diagnostic questions you should ask yourself. They'll help to determine if your innovation effort is heading in the right direction.

The first is this: has your CEO paid any attention whatsoever to your innovation efforts thus far? Is he or she even interested in the work you're doing?

If the answer is negative, you are potentially facing some difficult waters. CEO support for innovation has, in too many studies to mention here, been shown to be *the* critical success factor in getting new things done.

Of course, there are two reasons your CEO might not be noticing your efforts. The first is you're following a Play-Not-2-Lose innovation strategy, and have consequently focused on incrementalism. In this case you may not have a problem, because CEO attention will come with time as mounting returns follow from innovation at scale.

On the other hand, if you're following a Play-2-Win strategy you do definitely have something to worry about if you aren't getting noticed by the CEO.

When you're executing a Play-2-Win strategy, the kinds of innovation you're doing are material to the long term fortunes of your firm. Lack of attention from the CEO means you are either not expected to succeed or that at some future time you'll be stopped from succeeding. This should be addressed now, or at least as soon as there is something substantial to talk about.

But what if you can't get CEO attention no matter what you do? Unless you have a very good reason, it is time to drown-the-puppy.

The second diagnostic question is this: do you have visibility of a pathway to predictable best-in-class returns? In other words, can you say when you will be able to demonstrate you are the best available investment for your organisation, and back this up with substantive figures?

If you aren't able to articulate a reasonable story around the money your innovation programme will likely face significant challenge in the near term. The challenge will arise the moment the initial euphoria accompanying an innovation effort wears off. Then, business-as-usual investments will take precedence simply because they are seen as more certain.

The third and final diagnostic question to be asking at this point in the innovation effort is this: how much innovation is getting done entirely by the innovation team members, and how much by people outside the innovation team?

As I mentioned earlier in this book, one really needs to ensure that participative innovation is the ordinary operating mode for an innovation team. Doing innovation any other way means the innovation effort won't scale, which has the consequence of failing to generate appropriate financial results.

By the end of the first year, a solid and loyal base of innovation supporters should exist in your organisation. They'll be the ones who come up with ideas and who work on those ideas collaboratively. Their efforts will cause others to fight the innovation corner as well.

If you are in the lucky position of having satisfactory answers to all three of these diagnostic questions, there remains one further note: don't expect results too soon. Neither should you set an expectation that results will come quickly.

Innovation Management is a voyage of discovery. Successful innovation teams are built in years, not a few months.

Although I've stated throughout this book that an innovation effort has limited time between start and cancellation if it fails to generate significant returns, there is no point hiding the reality that it takes *time* to build those returns. There is no better advice I can give than to suggest you set the expectations of your management appropriately.

The first year or so of any innovation effort is a fragile, nervous time. You skate between hoping for the wins you must have and managing the politics which attend the times when you've had to drown-the-puppy for whatever reason.

Every week it seems, a new challenge raises its head that has to be handled personally and carefully. The innovation team always seem to be walking on thin ice.

This scenario changes the longer you persist in your innovation effort. Eventually, you get to a tipping point beyond which the possibility of cancellation is remote. Time and time again, I have seen organisations reach that tipping point when their innovation efforts have gotten predictable and become just another business-as-usual process.

It takes time, but the tipping point always arrives eventually with perseverance.

Thank you for taking the time to read *The Little Innovation Book*. I hope it has helped in some small way, your innovation efforts and the fortunes of your organisations.

About the Author

FORMERLY HEAD OF Innovation and CIO of Investment at Lloyds Banking Group in London, James Gardner is now Chief Technology Officer at the Department for Work and Pensions in the UK Government.

After studying Economics and Computer Science in Australia, he acquired his doctorate for research on the simulation of innovation diffusion pre-market. He then went on to work on a range of first-of-a-kind innovations in financial services and in other industries. After a stint at Microsoft Australia in their financial services practice, he moved to London to work for Lloyds Banking Group.

James has also worked in the telecommunications, software, and education sectors.

James is the author of banking best-seller *Innovation and the Future-Proof Bank*, and publishes regularly on his blog. He is presently writing his third book, *How Hits Work*, to be published in 2011. *How Hits Work* argues that companies who create hit products rarely do so because they have been especially innovative in their own right.

He currently resides in London, but travels around the world regularly visiting companies as a speaker and consultant.

Index

www.ingramcontent.com/pod-product-compliance
Lightning Source LLC
Chambersburg PA
CBHW060040210326
41520CB00009B/1207